I HEAR YOU

Eastwood Atwater, Ph.D. (University of Chicago), is a professor of psychology at Montgomery County Community College in suburban Philadelphia, Pennsylvania. He also has a private practice in psychology and leads workshops on communication skills. He is the author of *The Psychology of Adjustment* and a forthcoming book on *The Psychology of Adolescence*, both published by Prentice-Hall.

How to Use
Listening Skills for Profit

Eastwood Atwater

A SPECTRUM BOOK

PRENTICE-HALL, INC., Englewood Cliffs, New Jersey 07632

Library of Congress Cataloging in Publication Data
Atwater, Eastwood (date)
    I hear you.

    "A Spectrum Book."
    Includes bibliographical references and index.
    1. Communication in management.
    2. Communication in industrial relations.
    3. Listening.   4. Oral communication.   I. Title.
HD30.3.A9   658.4'52   81–17928
                            AACR2

ISBN 0-13-450684-7
ISBN 0-13-450676-6 {PBK.}

10   9   8   7   6   5   4   3   2   1

This Spectrum Book is available to businesses and organizations at a special discount when ordered in large quantities. For information, contact Prentice-Hall, Inc., General Publishing Division, Special Sales, Englewood Cliffs, N.J. 07632.

Prentice-Hall International, Inc., *London*
Prentice-Hall of Australia Pty. Limited, *Sydney*
Prentice-Hall of Canada, Ltd., *Toronto*
Prentice-Hall of India Private Limited, *New Delhi*
Prentice-Hall of Japan, Inc., *Tokyo*
Prentice-Hall of Southeast Asia Pte. Ltd., *Singapore*
Whitehall Books Limited, *Wellington, New Zealand*

CONTENTS

vii

PREFACE

Whenever people are promoted to positions of greater rewards and responsibilities, whether in business or other fields, it is usually because they have excelled in their given line of work. Once in that position, however, these people discover they need more than their special knowledge and expertise. They must also be adept in communicating and dealing with people. They need to express themselves clearly and to listen accurately to others. Yet of all the communication skills listening is the most demanding and the least mastered.

Much that is written on the subject simply stresses the importance of listening. This book is unique in that it focuses on *how* to listen. Throughout the following pages we will explain the attitudes and techniques for effective listening, together with specific suggestions and exercises for improving your own listening habits. The dos and don'ts of listening are summarized in the final chapter as a handy guide for your future reference.

As a practicing psychologist and consultant I want to thank the many people I've worked with, especially for their favorable response in improving their listening habits which has further encouraged my own interest in this area. I'd also like to thank my wife Kay for her help throughout the writing of this book and for the many valuable experiences we've shared in learning how to listen.

Eastwood Atwater

I HEAR YOU

CHAPTER ONE

THE FAILURE TO LISTEN

The famous novelist and philosopher André Gide once began a lecture by saying, "All this has been said before, but since nobody listened, it must be said again." How often this is true! So many things we hear go in one ear and out the other. Studies of the listening ability of thousands of people, including business and professional people, have shown that most of us fail to listen well. After listening to a ten-minute oral presentation, the average person understands and remembers only about half of what was said. Within forty-eight hours, up to one-half more is forgotten. In other words, you can expect to retain only one-fourth of what you heard someone say just a couple of days earlier.[1]

The failure to listen is the major cause of poor communication, resulting in needless misunderstanding, errors, and problems. Sometimes not listening can be hazardous, or even fatal, as when an airplane pilot fails to hear the control tower's warning of an approaching plane. This is why we begin a book on listening with a chapter on the failure to listen. We will start with a simple exercise to make you more aware of your own listening habits.

---

[1] *Your Personal Listening Profile* (booklet). Sperry Corporation, 1980.

HOW WELL DO YOU LISTEN?

Are you a careful listener? Or do you often have to ask people to repeat what they have said? Do you frequently misunderstand what you have heard?

To find out how well or poorly you listen you can do this simple exercise. The next time someone initiates a conversation with you, ask yourself "Am I really listening or am I just waiting my turn to talk?" With a corner of your awareness take stock of your own mental processes. Are you:

- easily distracted by other events?
- faking attention, or acting polite?
- reacting to emotional words?
- interrupting frequently?
- tuning out uninteresting topics?
- daydreaming, if the speaker is slow?
- jumping to conclusions?
- finding fault with the message?
- thinking of what you want to say?

How did you do? Were you surprised? The more of these you find yourself doing while someone is talking to you, the less you are really listening.

If you have difficulty doing this exercise while someone is talking with you, try doing it just after the conversation, while it is still fresh in your mind. Or, try doing it during a telephone conversation, when you won't be distracted by facial expressions, eye contact, or body language.

This exercise can make you more aware of your listening habits, and especially the difficulty of listening well. When people have been asked to rate themselves as listeners, more than 85 percent of them rate themselves as *average or worse*. Fewer than 5 percent rate themselves as "superior" or "excellent."[2] How would you rate yourself as a listener? How do you think others would rate you? You might ask your spouse, your best friends, and your boss or your subordinates at work for their opinions.

[2] *Ibid.*

2

WHY DON'T WE LISTEN?

Often we fail to listen because of some rather obvious reasons, such as being distracted or uninterested in what we hear. Sometimes we are simply too tired or too lazy to listen. After all, listening is hard work. But there are a number of other reasons why we fail to listen, which may or may not be as readily apparent as those listed. Let's take a look at these.

One reason we fail to listen is because we are too busy talking. Typically, when two friends meet on the street or at work, each is so eager to share his or her experiences that both may begin talking at once. What usually happens is that the partners "talk *at* each other," rather than listening and responding to what the other has said. As Nathan Miller aptly said, "Conversation in the United States is a competitive exercise in which the first person to draw a breath is declared the listener."[3] We might also add—a reluctant, frustrated listener who doesn't really listen at all.

A young woman, convinced that most people do not really listen to each other, decided to put her theory to test. During a cocktail party she said to another woman in her cheery, cocktail-party voice, "By the way, just before leaving the house, I shot my husband." "Oh, really?" came the reply. "How nice for you, dear." So it goes with so much of our everyday "ritual" communication. This is probably why you are not surprised when others do not remember things you have said at social gatherings. You write it off as "small talk." In contrast, you may be favorably impressed when someone does follow through with a request or promise made at such occasions. It means that person was really *listening*.

Another reason we don't listen is the mistaken view that listening simply consists of not talking. Not so. People refrain from talking for many reasons. They may be politely waiting their turn to speak. Or they may be thinking of what they want to say next. Sometimes people are daydreaming. For example, college students in a psychology class were asked to record their momentary thoughts at various times throughout the course with the following results:

---

[3] Quoted by Robert Bolton, *People Skills* (Englewood Cliffs, N.J.: Prentice-Hall, Inc., 1979), p. 4.

- 20 percent were paying attention, though only 12 percent were actively listening
- 20 percent were pursuing erotic thoughts
- 20 percent were reminiscing about something
- The rest were daydreaming, worrying, pondering religious thoughts, or thinking of lunch.[4]

Listening is an active process of paying attention to what is being said. As such, listening requires continual effort and concentration on what is being said. Yet listening does not preclude talking. Otherwise, how could we have two-way communication? Actually, a person who talks a lot may also be a good listener, especially if he or she is really interested in what the speaker is saying, pays attention, and knows how to process information well.

One of the most common causes of not listening is the preoccupation with one's self. The more wrapped up people are in their own feelings, needs, and problems, the less they are able to listen to others. Patients who are anxious about their health problem may misinterpret their physician's warnings or reassurances. Customers complaining about a defective product may hear only what they want to hear, at least until their irritation subsides. Couples about to marry characteristically ignore warnings and suggestions about their marriage, no matter how well-intentioned these may be. Business personnel, enthusiastic about their plans for a new product or program, often shut out potentially valuable criticism and suggestions, lest these interfere with their plans. In sum, people often fail to listen at the critical times in their lives when they most need to listen.

Sometimes people fail to listen because they don't really want to hear. I once got that feeling when I walked into a police chief's office where a desk placard read "Don't confuse me with the facts, my mind is made up." Sure enough, he was an opinionated person who did all the talking. I was just glad I was there on official business, and not someone in trouble with the law.

Each of us may refuse to listen at some times more than others. We may be less likely to give someone a fair hearing when

---

[4] Ron Adler and Neil Towne, *Looking Out/Looking In* (San Francisco: Rinehart Press, 1975), p. 171.

we feel highly emotional or opinionated about something. Or we may be afraid to hear something we do not want to hear when we feel anxious and insecure. We are also unlikely to hear very well whenever we feel we are an expert on something and have all the answers. Salespeople eager to make a sale may talk past a new customer, only to discover the latter's real needs after their presentation. Then too, all of us tend to bristle in the face of personal criticism, although this is the one time we could really benefit from listening.

Another common reason people don't listen is that they don't know how to listen. This shouldn't be surprising when you consider that people learn their listening habits primarily through personal example and imitation during the formative years. Those who grow up in families plagued by poor communication tend to repeat faulty listening habits—such as competitive talking, mistaking silence for listening, and judging too quickly. A woman paralyzed by the fear of criticism and failure once told me "People in my house are always blaming somebody."

Many people learn to listen only when they have to, or when they have discovered it is in their own best interests to do so. For example, couples seeking marriage counseling may learn for the first time how to listen to each other's feelings as a way of improving their communication. Parents seeking professional guidance for problems with their adolescents may discover the value, and learn the skill, of nonjudgmental listening. Busy managers and executives may also learn how to listen, not only to motivate their employees and resolve worker problems, but also in dealing with clients or customers. Fortunately, listening skills are now being taught more formally in a variety of courses such as Tom Gordon's courses in effectiveness training for parents, teachers, and business personnel.

One of the most common reasons we fail to listen is our tendency to be judgmental. After many years in clinical practice, psychologist Carl Rogers concluded that one of the major reasons we do not hear very well is "our very natural tendency to judge, to evaluate, to approve or disapprove the statements of the other person."[5]

[5] Carl R. Rogers, *On Becoming a Person* (Boston: Houghton Mifflin Company, 1961), p. 330.

Accordingly, we tend to judge anything and everything we see or hear, depending mostly on how it affects *us* personally. For example, if you have just seen an interesting program on television, you may find yourself thinking "I liked it" or "I didn't like it." If you ask a friend who saw the program, that person's response will usually express approval or disapproval, such as "I liked it, too," or "I didn't really care for it."

In other words, our first reaction is to judge things from our personal point of view. Yet more often than not, our judgmental responses interfere with good listening.

BARRIERS TO LISTENING

After teaching communication skills to thousands of parents, teachers, and businesspeople, Dr. Thomas Gordon has classified our evaluative remarks into a dozen different categories.[6] These are called "roadblocks to communication" and are illustrated below. Each time you and I use these commonplace responses, we tend to distort communication with others. As you read these responses, try to recall a situation in which you either used or heard them, and your feelings at the time.

ORDERING, DIRECTING, COMMANDING

Telling others to do something, like giving an order or command:

> "Say that again."
> "Slow down."
> "Don't speak to me like that."

WARNING, THREATENING, PROMISING

Telling others of the consequences which will follow if something is or is not done:

[6] From *Parent Effectiveness Training*. Wyden Books, New York, N.Y. Copyright 1970 Dr. Thomas Gordon. Used by permission.

"One more time and you are finished."
"Calm down, and I will listen."
"If you do that, you will be sorry."

MORALIZING, PREACHING, SHOULDS AND OUGHTS

Telling someone what he or she *ought* to do:

"You ought to go first."
"That's not right."
"You shouldn't act like that."

ADVISING, GIVING SUGGESTIONS OR SOLUTIONS

Giving advice, or telling someone how to solve a problem:

"Why don't you say so?"
"I would suggest you complain about it."
"Try doing it this way."

LECTURING, TEACHING, GIVING LOGICAL ARGUMENTS

Trying to influence someone with facts, arguments, or your own opinion:

"Look at it this way."
"You're in charge, it's your problem."
"When I was your age, I didn't have so much."

JUDGING, CRITICIZING, DISAGREEING, BLAMING

Making a negative judgment or evaluation of someone:

> "That was a foolish thing to do."
> "Now, you're on the right track."
> "I couldn't disagree with you more."
> "I told you that would happen."

PRAISING, AGREEING

Offering a positive evaluation:

> "I think you're right."
> "That was great."
> "We are proud of you."

NAME-CALLING, STEREOTYPING, SHAMING

Labeling other people, making them feel foolish:

> "Okay, Mr. Know-it-all."
> "All women drive like that."
> "You're acting like a dunce."

INTERPRETING, ANALYZING, DIAGNOSING

Telling people their motives, or analyzing why they are doing something:

> "You really don't believe that, do you?"
> "You're just saying that to bug me."
> "Now I know why you did that."

REASSURING, SYMPATHIZING, CONSOLING, SUPPORTING

Trying to make others feel better, talking them out of their feelings, denying the strength of their feelings:

"You will feel different next time."
"I used to feel that way too."
"Everyone makes mistakes."
"We are all behind you."

PROBING, QUESTIONING, INTERROGATING

Trying to find the reasons, motives, or causes of someone's behavior:

"When did you begin feeling this way?"
"Who gave you that idea?"
"What will you do the next time?"

WITHDRAWING, DISTRACTING, HUMORING

Trying to get others to look away from their problems, distracting or kidding them out of it:

"Why don't you forget it?"
"Let's talk about something else."
"Suppose you quit every time you fail?"

These responses are sometimes called the "dirty dozen" roadblocks to listening because of their disruptive effect on communication. They tend to interrupt the speaker and distract his or her train of thought. Most of them imply a desire to change, control, or modify the speaker. That is, they serve to take responsibility away from the speaker, and put the listener in charge. Because of that, these roadblocks invariably put speakers on the defensive, making them resistant and resentful. A defensive speaker then begins to defend and hide his or her ideas or feelings, rather than disclose them to us. The irony of all this is that we tend to use these roadblocks more out of habit than conscious intent. But the effect is the same—we fail to hear what the speaker is saying to us.

HAZARDS OF NOT LISTENING

So often it is said of people who get into trouble, "She simply wouldn't listen." The rebellious teenager comes first to mind, and the tragic example of the headstrong runaway who gets involved with "bad company." But it is not always the young who refuse to listen in these situations. Alice, a teenager who eventually died of an overdose of drugs, had written about her parents in her diary: "They talk, and they talk and they talk and talk, but never once did they even hear one thing I was trying to say."[7] Both parents had tried to help their daughter. But, at least from Alice's point of view, they couldn't help because they didn't know how to listen.

According to the TV re-enactment of the Jonestown tragedy, almost a thousand people committed suicide because of their leader's paranoia and refusal to listen. At one point, Jim Jones, the leader of the People's Temple, appealed to the Governor of Guyana for help. Yet he remained so headstrong that eventually the governor threw up his hands in desperation saying, "I cannot help you if you will not listen."

In another fatal example, we are told that the crew of the newly christened Titanic refused to listen to no less than *seven* warnings of icebergs on that fateful night of April 12, 1912. As a result, hundreds of people lost their lives needlessly. They had been led to believe the Titanic was "unsinkable." Even after the ship had struck the iceberg and was slowly sinking, most of the passengers refused to heed the captain's orders to get into the lifeboats. Comfortably housed on an upright ship with a dark, cold sea outside, they preferred to stay on board as long as possible. When the ship finally began listing dangerously just before sinking, it was too late. The only survivors were the people who had listened and taken to the lifeboats.

The cost of faulty listening in business is staggering. It has been estimated that if each of the 100 million workers in America makes a simple ten-dollar listening mistake, billions of dollars are wasted. Just think of the letters that must be retyped, the appoint-

[7] From the book, *Go Ask Alice.* Copyright 1971 by Prentice-Hall, Inc. Published by Prentice-Hall, Inc., Englewood Cliffs, N.J. 07632.

ments that must be rescheduled, and the shipments that must be reshipped, all because someone failed to listen. When people in large corporations fail to listen to each other, the costs are magnified. Information and ideas get distorted as they travel through the chain of command. Employees feel alienated from management, and the latter in turn feel more distant from top management.[8] I once heard a chief executive, newly appointed to a troubled company, give a stimulating presentation of the company's objectives, and then ask for some reaction. After an awkward silence, one manager said, "I think you are going to need our help in accomplishing these goals. But many of us feel discouraged about the company because your predecessor never listened to our ideas." Feeling rebuffed but regaining his composure, the executive wisely replied, "I agree. And I will try to do a better job listening to your ideas."

The refusal to listen to criticism and complaints can be especially devastating. For example, a manager once bragged to his employees that he put all customer complaints into a file marked "nuisance mail." He never bothered to answer these complaints, he explained, "because most of these people who call or write in are cranks. You can't please everybody. And besides, most of them aren't going to do anything more about their complaints anyway." You probably won't be surprised to learn that this manager was eventually fired for gross incompetence.

In contrast, a successful executive once told me, "Your critics can tell you where you are going wrong even before your friends can." Apparently, he had learned the folk wisdom attributed to the famous philosopher Leibnitz: "I would walk twenty miles to listen to my worst enemy if I could learn something." Listening to criticism may deflate the ego momentarily, but the failure to listen can be even more costly.

EXERCISES

HOW WELL DO YOU LISTEN?   Even though this exercise was given early in this chapter, we repeat it here, since it is so important.

[8] *Your Personal Listening Profile* (booklet). Sperry Corporation, 1980.

How often do you "wait for your turn to talk" rather than listen? To find out, the next time someone initiates a conversation with you, when it is convenient to do so, ask yourself how often you were:

- easily distracted by something else?
- faking attention, or acting polite?
- reacting to emotional words?
- interrupting frequently?
- tuning out dry subjects?
- daydreaming, if the speaker was slow?
- finding fault with the message?
- thinking of your own ideas?

The more of these you find yourself doing, the more you are simply waiting your turn to talk rather than listening.

OBSERVING LISTENING BEHAVIOR.   The next time it is convenient to do so, observe the listening behavior of two or three people in conversation. You might observe several friends sharing their experiences or a small staff meeting. But select a situation in which the participants are trying to communicate some information or their feelings to each other, rather than engaging in routine "small talk."

How well did the participants listen to each other? Using your observations, go back and answer the questions in the first exercise. That is, were the participants easily distracted? Were they faking attention? Were they reacting to emotional words? and so forth.

How frequently did the participants use the various roadblocks to communication? Which ones? Did each participant characteristically use some of these more than others? What was the effect of these judgmental responses on the communication?

Since it is usually easier to recognize the listening behavior of other people rather than our own, observing others is often a first step in becoming more aware of our own listening habits.

ROADBLOCKS TO LISTENING. Are you are aware of any *characteristic* faults in your listening habits? To find out, go back and familiarize yourself with the twelve types of roadblocks to listening. Do you tend to use some of these more than others? Which ones? Ask your friends, spouse, and colleagues for their impressions of your listening habits.

People who customarily use roadblocks 6 through 9 tend to be strongly judgmental. Those who habitually use roadblocks 1 through 4 plus 11 are too quick to solve other people's problems for them. And those who characteristically use roadblocks 5, 10, and 12 tend to avoid other people's concerns. Which of these categories best characterizes your responses? At the same time, bear in mind that each of us indulges in practically every one of these roadblocks at one time or another. The less often we use them, of course, the better we listen.

THE HAZARDS OF NOT LISTENING. Can you think of some instances in which people have suffered or hurt others by their failure to listen? Occasionally, of course, creative individuals may be glad they have persisted in their convictions despite the warnings or criticism of others. But more often than not, the refusal to listen results in needless disappointment, hurt, and failure, not only for those who do not listen but for others as well.

How about yourself? Have there been times you have been accused of "not listening" or being "headstrong"? Was there some truth to this? Did you later regret it? What were the circumstances? Were you being swept along by your emotions?

Ironically, we often resist listening to those we are the most emotionally involved with, and at the very times we most need to listen, during conflicts, problems, and decision-making.

CHAPTER TWO

FROM HEARING TO LISTENING

> We have been given two ears and but a single mouth, in order that we may listen more and talk less.
>
> —Zeno of Citium

Three-fourths of human communication consists of speaking and listening.[1] Yet, as we have noted, spoken messages are easily forgotten, and the failure to listen can be costly. As a result, people turn to memo-writing. Even the smallest detail becomes the subject of a memo, adding to the existing pile of paperwork and red tape. So often, speaking would be more appropriate than writing, if only people knew how to listen.

Listening is especially important in informal communication in which people express their *real* attitudes and feelings. This may be seen in the upward communication within business and professional circles. Management has many avenues to send messages downward; but there are few means for upward communication. The most obvious of these is the company "grapevine"—the chain of people talking to people. The worker talks to the supervisor, who in turn talks to the manager, and so it goes from person to person until the message eventually reaches the top, fragmented and distorted though it may be. Unfortunately, managers often set a poor example by failing to listen. They announce that their doors are always open, but then fail to listen. Too often they do

[1] *Your Personal Listening Profile.* Sperry Corporation, 1980.

not know how to listen. After experiencing repeated frustration in expressing their grievances or suggestions, subordinates avoid taking advantage of the manager's offer, shutting off a valuable two-way flow of communication.

In this chapter we will look at the characteristics of listening as an active process, along with an overview of the various listening skills discussed in the book. Then we will describe the elementary but often overlooked skills associated with giving your physical attention to another person. Finally, we will look at the different styles of listening, including status and role differences.

HEARING AND LISTENING

Perhaps a good place to begin is with the distinction between hearing and listening. According to Webster's *New World Dictionary,* to listen is "to make a conscious effort to hear" or "to pay attention" to sound. Right away, you will notice that listening is more than hearing. Essentially, hearing pertains to the physical reception of sound, listening to the perception of *meaningful* sound. Hearing is an automatic reaction of the senses and nervous system. Listening is a voluntary act, involving our higher mental processes as well. You have to want to listen. Otherwise you will hear only what you want or need to hear, rather than what has been said, which happens all too often.

We hear many things, of course, but we listen to only a few of them. Our ears become so bombarded by sounds that we block out of our conscious attention everything except the sounds that interest us at the moment. We become so accustomed to the commonplace sounds of our surroundings that we no longer pay attention to them, though others do. For example, city people gradually ignore the noise of passing trucks and trains, though newcomers to town may be bothered by them. Similarly, country people ignore the crickets, while city people may be fascinated by their sound. In both cases, people ignore the common sounds of their surroundings and are more apt to notice sounds when they change, cease, or are deliberately brought to their attention.

This was brought home to me one summer evening while

my wife and I were sitting on our porch. I was paying attention to our conversation, with little awareness of the usual sounds of the evening. Suddenly my wife said, "Listen to the crickets." Sure enough, as I consciously turned my attention to the crickets, I heard them. Of course, I had been hearing them all along, since hearing is an automatic, involuntary act, but I became fully aware of their sound only as I consciously *listened* to them.

What about the effect of noise on our hearing? Noise is usually taken to mean loud, unpleasant, or confusing sound. We are all familiar with the immediate effects of noise: Our muscles become tense, our stomachs become jittery, our eyes blink. We may even jump. Noise is stressful in that it affects our performance. We cannot think and make decisions as quickly or accurately in a noisy environment.

Surprisingly, people readily adapt to noise. When two groups of subjects were exposed to very loud noise and no noise respectively, results showed that the noise produced physiological and behavioral effects. But such effects disappeared within three or four minutes, with subjects exposed to the loud noise performing as well as those with no noise. While simple tasks like matching telephone numbers or even higher level math problems seem unaffected by noise, other tasks are adversely affected, such as the constant monitoring of a dial, or attempting to perform two tasks at once. Thus, a person who is already having difficulty concentrating on a task and trying to perform at maximum capacity is more likely to be adversely affected by loud noise.[2]

It seems that people are more apt to be bothered by noise that is unpredictable and beyond their control, like the screeching of tires at busy intersections. Also, prolonged exposure to noise is more likely to disturb hearing and listening. At least this is what came out of a study of residents in an apartment house built over a busy highway in New York City. Noise levels were especially high because of the design of the building, with the sounds of cars and trucks traveling through open vents in the buildings. The noise level was much higher on the lower floors, with a decibel reading of sixty-six on the eighth floor, twice as high as that on

[2] D. C. Glass and J. E. Singer, *Urban Stress.* New York: Academic Press, 1972.

the thirty-second floor. An investigation of children who had lived in the building four or more years found that there was a definite relationship between the floors on which the children lived and their hearing and reading ability. Children on the lower eleven floors were much more likely to exhibit poor hearing ability (the discrimination of auditory sounds) and also were in the lower levels of reading ability. The point is that it is difficult to listen accurately in a noisy environment.[3]

LISTENING IS AN ACTIVE PROCESS

Listening is made possible because of the lag between the spoken word and the mental activity of the listener. Ordinarily, people speak about 125 words per minute, though we can listen at about three to four times that rate, or four hundred words per minute. Yet the lag that makes listening possible in the first place can also lead us astray, especially if the speaker is slow or uninteresting. We may soon find ourselves not paying attention, for listening is an active, but internal process. As such, listening presupposes that we want to listen, that we pay attention, and that we share responsibility with the speaker.

First of all, we must *want* to listen. Otherwise, the speaker's words fall on deaf ears, as so often happens. I recall a friend of mine whose mother would call out to him to "take out the trash." He said he first had to ask himself, "Did I hear my mother?" Sometimes, when he was tired or busy doing something else, he had trouble "hearing" her. He heard his mother only when he wanted to hear her. Simplistic as that sounds, it happens to all of us at one time or another. How often have we listened to someone speak when we were not interested or were tired. We listened only half-heartedly. Then when someone asks us what was said, our mind goes blank. It turns out that we heard very little of what was said because we were not really listening, mostly because we didn't want to.

[3] S. Cohen, D. C. Glass, and J. E. Singer, "Apartment Noise, Auditory Discrimination, and Reading Ability in Children," *Journal of Experimental Social Psychology*, 1975, 9, 407–422.

We must also *pay attention*. Small wonder that we use the word "pay" here, which implies giving something for something else in exchange. Ordinarily we speak of paying in monetary terms, but in listening we pay out our most personal and intimate treasure, our awareness, our interest, and our effort, in order to receive something in return—a meaning, information, understanding, or perhaps comfort or entertainment. Listening is hard work, which is why we do not give our attention indiscriminately. And above all, listening is a gift. It has been described as one of the greatest gifts we can give each other. When people feel they have been deprived of listening, especially when troubled, they are often willing to pay money to be listened to by professionals.

Listening is an active process in another sense, in that we must *share the responsibility* for communication with the speaker. Henry Thoreau once said, "It takes two to speak the truth—one to speak, and another to hear." Listeners and speakers alike bear 100 percent of the responsibility for the communication. Often we fail to exercise our responsibility as listeners because we are tired or uninterested in what is being said. Or we may have a closed mind. Many times we are not sufficiently active in trying to understand the speaker. For example, perhaps you have asked someone for street directions. But no sooner do you start off than you become uncertain of the directions you were just given. Usually you blame the person who gave them to you, though more often than not you share in the blame. Perhaps you failed to be sufficiently active in the listening process.

Another example is the common misunderstanding between doctors and patients. A study by graduate students at Case Western Reserve University showed a wide disparity between what physicians intended to say and what patients heard them say. The doctor's remark "It will only hurt a little," was taken to mean anything from a quick pinch to some discomfort. Yet 22 percent of the patients, compared with only 2 percent of the doctors, said it meant a lot of pain. Furthermore, only about half the doctors and patients took the phrase "going home from the hospital soon" to mean two to four days. Yet among the others, three times as many patients as doctors thought it meant "tomorrow," setting the stage for misunderstanding. A major implication of this study is that patients should assume more responsibility in communicating with their doctors. They must ask questions when they do not understand just what the doctor means.[4]

Listening is also an active process in the sense that it requires the use of *learned skills.* Are you surprised at this? Actually, listening is the communication skill learned first and used most often. Yet, of all the communication skills, it is the least taught and least mastered.[5] Consequently, as we have seen, most people are inefficient listeners. But it doesn't have to be this way. Each of us can listen more effectively through *learning* how to listen.

The major goal of this book is to help you become a better listener through understanding the attitudes and skills needed for listening. Some of these skills are rather obvious and tangible, such as the use of eye contact and positive gestures. Other skills are less apparent and have to do more with our attitude and understanding, such as our acceptance and empathy toward the speaker. All of these skills may be grouped into various clusters of related listening skills, as seen in Table 1. We will devote a separate chapter to each cluster, with the exception of the attending skills, which will be discussed in the following section on "Total Body Listening."

TOTAL BODY LISTENING

This has to do with giving your physical attention to another person. When I am especially eager to hear something, like the latest news or bit of spicy gossip, I may tell the speaker "I'm all ears." What I mean is that I intend to give the speaker my undivided attention. I do this by adopting a bodily posture of listening—facing the speaker, establishing eye contact, and paying attention. Such total body listening not only expresses my readiness to listen with my ears, but also aids in the act of listening itself. Although we may adopt total body listening unconsciously, for the most part, we can consciously use these attending skills as a way of enhancing

[4] Associated Press release, in *The Philadelphia Inquirer,* November **27,** 1980.
[5] *Your Personal Listening Profile.* Sperry Corporation, 1980.

TABLE 1
CLUSTERS OF LISTENING SKILLS[6]

Attending skills	Minimizing distractions Attentiveness Eye contact Positive body language
Following or nonreflective listening skills	Attentive silence Conversation starters Minimal responses Infrequent questions
Reflective listening skills	Clarifying Paraphrasing Reflecting feelings Summarizing
Essential attitudes	Acceptance Self-acceptance Empathy
Nonverbal communication skills	Interpreting— Facial expressions Gazing and eye contact Vocal expressions Posture and gestures Personal space
Memory skills	Concentration Short-term memory Long-term memory

our listening behavior. Total body listening requires that we minimize distractions, pay attention, maintain eye contact, and use positive body language.

MINIMIZE DISTRACTIONS.   It is important to block out everything that may distract us from listening. If we meet someone in a crowded place, like an auditorium or restaurant, it is wise to step aside and find a "quiet corner." If we are in a home, turning off the television or stereo can greatly reduce distractions. If we are in an office, it helps to ask someone else to answer the phone when it rings, or ask not to be disturbed. Nothing is so distracting

[6] From the book, *People Skills*, by Robert Bolton. Copyright © 1979 by Prentice-Hall, Inc. Englewood Cliffs, N.J. 07632. Published by Prentice-Hall, Inc.

as being interrupted every few minutes by someone's telephone or secretary. While we may be duly impressed by how busy the other person is, we cannot help feeling like an unwanted intruder. In such a situation, if the speaker isn't sufficiently sensitive to these matters, the listener may ask "Is it possible to talk with you in private without being disturbed?" The speaker should get the point.

PAY ATTENTION. This is so obvious you may wonder why we bother to mention it. The reason is because it is the hardest part of listening, and that is why so many of us listen so poorly. Psychologists have discovered that our attention is constantly shifting. This is why television ads keep changing so quickly from one image to another, to keep our attention. And mind you, this is true for our *visual* attention, which is our primary mode of learning. Attending to a *verbal* message is even more demanding, especially when there are few or no visual aids, as in telephone conversation. Yet paying attention actually heightens our ability to listen. Paying attention produces "expectancy waves" in the brain, making us more alert to what follows.

You may be interested to discover that paying attention also aids the speaker, another reminder that the listener shares responsibility for communication with the speaker. In public speaking, as well as in private discourse, experimental studies have shown that when listeners change from deliberately ignoring speakers to paying attention to them, speakers tend to increase their rate of speech, use more gestures, and "come alive" in communicating their message.

ESTABLISH EYE CONTACT. Maintaining eye contact with the speaker not only shows we are interested, but also encourages the speaker to continue and in turn helps us to pay better attention. The next time someone initiates a conversation with you, notice what both of you do with your eyes. How much is the speaker looking at you? How much are you gazing back in turn? You may discover that as a listener you are likely to be looking at the speaker more than vice versa. You may also discover that the natural, spontaneous pattern in most conversations is for each person to establish eye contact briefly, then momentarily glance aside, then reestablish eye contact, repeating this pattern throughout the conversation. Occasionally, someone may read a book on body language or impression formation and discover that others are more likely to form a favorable impression of us when we look them in the eye. Then they proceed to overdo a good thing, making the speaker (or listener as the case may be) feel uncomfortable. For example, constant eye contact may be interpreted as staring, which in turn signals hostility, especially in competitive situations. The ideal, instead, is to strive for optimum rather than maximum eye contact, that which feels natural and comfortable to both parties, and is appropriate to the situation and transaction.

USE POSITIVE BODY LANGUAGE. Since most of our communicating is nonverbal, positive body language expresses our desire to listen. Sitting toward the front of your chair and leaning forward with an animated expression is a way of saying "I'm all ears." On the other hand, slouching down in your chair expresses a casual, disinterested attitude. Standing with folded arms goes along with a defensive attitude, and putting hands on your hips shows a defiant attitude. When listeners show little or no body movement, especially without eye contact, a speaker may wonder if the listener is "still there." Speakers usually prefer listeners with responsive body language, though an overly fidgety listener may distract the speaker. There is also a tendency for listeners unconsciously to mimic the speaker's posture and gestures, as if to say "I'm with you." Other matters, like sitting or standing too close or too far away, may also enhance or interfere with our verbal communication, and will be explored in greater detail in a later chapter on "The Importance of Nonverbal Communication."

LISTENING STYLES

Body language, eye contact, and paying attention are all aids to good listening, but they are used in different ways by each of us. Just as there are individual styles of walking, talking, and looking, so are there individual styles of listening.

Your own characteristic style of listening is an expression

of who you are—your personality, your interests and concerns, your status and sex. The way in which we listen to someone also depends on situational factors, such as whether we are on the job or at home, in a hurry or relaxing, and so forth. In fact, good listening implies sufficient flexibility to adjust our listening style to both the person and the situation. But aside from these expected variations, most of us exhibit a characteristic style of listening.

In the first place, listening styles vary in terms of how judgmental or understanding we are. The noted clinical psychologist, Dr. Carl Rogers, found that 80 percent of all verbal communication involved five types of responses: evaluative, interpretive, supportive, probing, and understanding.[7] The other 20 percent was incidental and insignificant to communication. Evaluative, judgmental responses were the most common, as we noted in the opening chapter. Interpretive, supportive, and probing remarks were decreasingly common in that order. Understanding responses were the least common of all. Rogers found that when someone used the same type of response at least 40 percent of the time, people saw that person as *always* responding that way.

Can you think of friends or associates who characteristically listen in each of these ways? Judgmental listeners say things like "That's good" or "That's wrong." Interpretive listeners are more likely to say things like "You're saying that to make me feel guilty" or "Now I know why you said that." Supportive listeners are quick to agree or sympathize with the speaker, with remarks like "You're absolutely right" or "I feel sorry for you." Probing listeners, on the other hand, are more apt to say "When?" or "Give me a specific example." You may recall that Thomas Gordon has characterized these first four types of responses as "roadblocks" to communication. Understanding listeners, however, are more likely to make good use of attentive silence and reflective, empathetic responses, as explained in the next two chapters.

How about your own listening habits? Do you tend to adopt some of these listening responses more than others? If so, which ones? If in doubt, ask your friends how they see your characteristic style of listening. You may be surprised.

[7] In David W. Johnson, *Reaching Out.* Englewood Cliffs, N.J.: Prentice-Hall, Inc., 1972, p. 129.

Listening styles also vary in terms of status and relative positions of the speaker and listener. An example is the familiar television commercial "When E. F. Hutton talks, people listen." We generally listen best to those who have more status or seniority than we do, especially when we have something to gain from it. On the other hand, people of higher status do not always return the favor. In a conversation between people of different status or rank, the higher status person is more likely to interrupt the conversation than to hear the person out. For example, managers interrupt workers more frequently than vice versa. How about your own experience? Do you get the feeling that people of higher status really listen to what you are saying? Or are they merely acting polite? And how well do you listen to those of lower social status or rank? Do you hear them out? Or do you frequently interrupt them to "get on" with what *you* want to say?

In many instances our characteristic listening style is affected by sex-role differences. Two researchers taped a number of private conversations and discovered important differences between men and women. When two men or two women are talking, the number of interruptions between partners is about the same. But when a man and a woman are talking, the man makes about 96 percent of the interruptions. About a third of the time, women make "retrievals," attempts to pick up the line of the conversation from the point where they were interrupted.[8]

It seems that men tend to concentrate more on the content of the conversation, while women tend to pay more attention to the process. A man usually listens to what is being said for about the first ten or fifteen seconds. Then he begins to "self-listen," to see what he can add to the conversation. Dr. Warren Farrell holds that this self-listening is a male-conditioned habit, in which men have been trained to add to the substance of the conversation and to become problem-solvers.[9] Of course, when a man does this, he stops listening and concentrates on breaking in instead. As a result, men tend to enter a conversation too quickly with a ready

[8] *Time* magazine, September 25, 1978.
[9] Jack Houston, "Men, Women Don't Listen the Same," *The Philadelphia Inquirer*, February 24, 1976, p. 2-C. From a speech given by Dr. Warren Farrell at the American Management Association Personnel Conference in Chicago, February, 1976.

answer. They fail to draw out the speaker with questions or to listen for more information before coming to a conclusion. Men also tend to be fault-finders, leaping on an error in the substance of a conversation rather than waiting for the good points as well.

Women, on the other hand, tend to listen more to the person—who is speaking? who is left out?—and the feelings being expressed. As mentioned before, they are also less likely to interrupt the speaker and more likely to attempt retrievals.

This doesn't necessarily mean that all men are insensitive interrupters, nor that all women are warm and receptive listeners. Far from it. It simply means that men and women are socialized differently, and insofar as individual men and women are shaped by sterotyped sex roles they *may* exhibit the listening styles just described. But there are numerous exceptions among both sexes. Men who work with people—psychiatrists, psychologists, social workers, teachers—often listen in ways that combine the desirable characteristics of both men and women. Similarly, women who have positions of responsibiliy may not only listen to the feelings of their partners, but also can propose constructive solutions to problems as well.

As members of each sex become freer to acquire communication skills without restrictive sex-role connotations, their overall effectiveness may improve to fit the task at hand. Men and women alike are discovering that good communication and sensitivity to human relationships—including listening—become increasingly important as one goes up the ladder of responsibility in any field.

At this point you may be wondering about the possibilities for changing your own listening habits. You will be pleased to discover that people have shown marked improvements in listening after only a minimum of training. Simply reading a book like this is a good beginning. Doing the exercises and practicing your listening skills in everyday communication is even better. Attending a seminar or a course in communication skills may also help. People taking a course in listening comprehension have as much as doubled their listening skills in just a few months.[10] Such an improvement in listening in turn leads to better communication and performance

[10] *Your Personal Listening Profile.* Sperry Corporation, 1980.

on the job. As Calvin Coolidge, former president of the United States, once said, "Nobody ever listened himself out of a job."

EXERCISES

THE LISTENING GAME. This can be done alone, but it is more interesting with someone else. Close your eyes and mentally list all the different sounds you hear during a period of about one minute. If you are in a noisy, busy place you can make the time shorter; if it is a quiet place you could allow more time.

Now open your eyes and compare your lists of sounds. Did you both hear the same sounds? If there were any sounds that one of you heard but the other didn't, was it because of better attentiveness, "sharper" ears, concentration, or perhaps greater selectivity?

This exercise demonstrates that keen attention is the single most essential attribute of good listening. It also shows how unaware we can be of the sounds around us until we consciously begin to pay attention to them.

TOTAL BODY LISTENING. The next time it is convenient, observe two people having a conversation with the following questions in mind:

- To what extent are the partners listening with their entire bodies?
- Are they really paying attention to each other? How can you tell? Are they distracted in any way?
- Do the partners maintain eye contact? Do they alternate between looking at and looking away from each other? Does each person look more while listening than speaking?
- Are the partners using positive body language? Do they adopt an open stance toward each other? Or do they fold their arms, or place their hands on their hips?
- Do their body postures and gestures help or hinder their listening?

You may choose to observe the behavior of someone who is listening to you. Or you may become more aware of your own listening behavior while others are speaking to you. In either case, the aim of this exercise is to make you more aware of how total body listening may aid in communication.

YOUR LISTENING STYLE.   This exercise is based on **Carl Rogers'** study of the five types of verbal responses in communication, discussed earlier in the chapter. You may recall that evaluative responses were the most common, with interpretive, supportive, and probing remarks decreasingly common in this order. Understanding responses were the least common of all. How do these responses apply to you?

- Are you characteristically a judgmental listener, making responses such as "That's good" or "That's right"?
- Do you also find yourself making interpretive responses such as "I know why you said that"?
- Are you inclined to make supportive responses, such as "I feel sorry for you"?
- Do you use probing responses like "When?" or "Why?"
- Do you sometimes make understanding responses, without the roadblocks to listening discussed in the first chapter?

Rogers observed that when anyone relies on one of these responses at least 40 percent of the time, people see that person *always* responding this way. Do you characteristically use some of these responses more than others? If so, which ones? Ask your friends how they see you.

OBSERVING MEN AND WOMEN.   While reading this chapter, have you become aware of any differences between men's and women's listening habits? You can conduct the following exercise to see for yourself. For practical purposes, an "interruption" occurs when one person begins speaking before the other has finished. A "retrieval" takes place when one of them attempts to pick up the thread of the conversation at the point where an interruption occurred.

First, observe several same-sex pairs in conversation. Then observe several opposite-sex pairs talking. Using a scorecard like the one shown, count all the interruptions and retrievals by each person. Since people in higher status positions usually interrupt more frequently, select people of the same social status or position to rule out this effect.

Did you find that men tend to interrupt more frequently than women? Did women make more retrieval responses?

If you find that your observations differ from those described in this book, it may be because of individual styles or the small number of people involved in your exercise.

	MAN	WOMAN	WOMAN A	WOMAN B	MAN A	MAN B
INTERRUPTIONS	卌	||	||	卌 ||	卌 卌	卌
RETRIEVALS			|||	|||		||	卌	

SELF-AWARENESS OF SEX-ROLES DIFFERENCES.   To what extent do the stereotyped sex-role differences in listening apply to you?

If you are a man, do you think you frequently interrupt others? If you are a woman, do you think you are more likely to make retrievals than interruptions? Try to become more aware of your own listening style in future conversations. You can also ask those who know you for their observations of your listening habits.

It is well to remember that individuals of both sexes vary greatly among themselves in terms of their listening styles, depending on many factors, including the extent to which they have been influenced by the sex-role stereotypes. Then too, personal and occupational experiences make a difference, with those of either sex who work with people usually being more skilled in listening. Do you know individuals who do not fit these stereotypes?

CHAPTER THREE

NONREFLECTIVE LISTENING

Up to this point we have described listening as an active process, involving an attitude of caring as well as mental and bodily attention.

We have also noted that most of us do not know how to listen. We tend to judge, probe, or analyze what others say to us. We are preoccupied more with our own concerns than with those of others. We also tend to interrupt the speaker. Poor listening habits such as these have a way of distorting the message. Even worse, they often cut off the flow of communication completely.

Because so many "listening" faults are committed through our voiced responses to the speaker, a simple way to avoid them is by saying little or nothing. Without relinquishing either our caring attitude or our attention, we can use the simple strategy of nonreflective listening.

WHAT IS NONREFLECTIVE LISTENING?

Essentially, this is the simplest form of listening. It consists of making good use of *attentive silence* and *minimal* vocal responses, like "mm-hmm." Sometimes nonreflective listening is called "passive" listening, even though we have explained that all listening is an active process in terms of being attentive both psychologically and physically. When appropriate, nonreflective listening may communicate acceptance, understanding, and reassurance. Sometimes nonreflective listening is our only choice, for example, when speakers are eager to express their viewpoints, especially when they are emotionally aroused or have difficulty saying what's on their mind. In these instances, they have a need to talk and be heard, without counting on a specific response from us.

For example, suppose someone has just been given an unexpected work assignment and comes to complain about it. Also, suppose you, as the manager, respond to his complaints with some of the typical roadblocks to communication as follows:

> Jim: Aw, come on. This is the last thing I need. I mean, this is just too much.
>
> Manager: You're always complaining.
>
> Jim: Well, I don't think it's fair. I'm always getting these special handouts.
>
> Manager: Yeah, we all know you're being persecuted. Now get to work.

As you would surmise, such a routine complaint could quickly escalate into a heated emotional exchange, creating a lot of misunderstanding and resentment on both sides. By responding to Jim's complaints with judgmental, sarcastic remarks, the manager not only antagonizes Jim but also fails to learn *why* he is complaining so loudly. The manager mistakenly sees Jim's complaint as a challenge to authority and puts him down.

Instead, suppose the manager recognizes Jim's need to ventilate his feelings and engages in nonreflective listening. The conversation might go something like this:

> Jim: Aw, come on. This is the last thing I need. I mean, this is just too much
>
> Manager: Oh?
>
> Jim: Yeah, I've already got so many other things hanging fire in my regular work.
>
> Manager: How's that?
>
> Jim: I mean two of our regular suppliers have just gone on

strike, leaving our West Coast dealers in real trouble.
I'm already having to put in extra time on this as it is.
I don't think I can handle all this new stuff too.

Manager: Mmmm—I see.

The manager's willingness to engage in nonreflective listening, especially in the early part of this conversation, helps to uncover some of the reasons for Jim's complaint. It isn't really that Jim is challenging his boss's authority, but that Jim feels temporarily overwhelmed by his other responsibilities, which his manager had not been fully aware of. By not interrupting, but simply listening for just a few minutes, the manager comes to a new level of understanding of Jim. Whether or not the manager has a change of mind and assigns the new job to someone else, both parties will come away from this exchange with more understanding and respect for each other.

LISTENING WITH MINIMAL RESPONSES

In the above example, notice how the manager responded with succinct phrases like "Oh?" "How's that?" and "I see." Such phrases are referred to variously as neutral responses, minimal responses, or door-openers. Whatever we choose to call them, they all have one thing in common—namely, they are noncoercive invitations to talk. Accordingly, they help to communicate acceptance, interest, and understanding where sheer silence would not.

Sometimes we can take our cue from the speaker's nonverbal expression. That is, a person's tone of voice, facial expression, posture, or movement tells us he or she has something to say. When this is so, we can facilitate conversation merely by saying things like:

- You look happy.
- Is something bothering you?
- You seem preoccupied.
- Worried about something?

- You look jumpy.
- What's wrong?

The most commonly used response is the familiar "Mm-hmm," a simple, nonobtrusive sound which communicates "I'm interested." Studies have shown that saying "Mm-hmm" or simply nodding one's head has the effect of encouraging the speaker to talk for a longer period of time.[1] Of course, there are many other responses that may serve the same purpose. Whenever possible, you should use those that come to you naturally, as long as they are truly "neutral" or nonjudgmental. Some commonly used minimal responses are:

- Yeah?
- Go on.
- I see.
- Oh?
- I'd like to hear.
- Tell me more.
- Explain that?
- Wow!
- Really?

Because these responses are neutral or nonjudgmental, they are sometimes called "door-openers." That is, they help to facilitate conversation, especially in the beginning. Such comments also provide encouragement to the speaker in a way that mere silence would not. While silence may be very meaningful and satisfying among close friends, it is often misconstrued as a sign of disinterest or rejection among people who do not know each other well. Hence, the value of the *minimal* response, just enough to sustain the flow of self-expression.

Sometimes, however, people may unwittingly use short responses in a more coercive, manipulative way, that is, as roadblocks to communication. Some examples are:

[1] J. D. Matarazzo, A. N. Wiens, and G. Saslow, "Studies of Interview Speech Behavior," in L. Krasner and L. P. Ullman (Eds.), *Research in Behavior Modification.* New York: Holt, Rinehart & Winston, 1965.

- What's on your mind?
- Why?
- Just give me three reasons.
- Why not?
- Oh, it can't be that bad.
- Aw, come on.
- Cheer up.

As you readily see, these remarks will most likely have the effect of either shutting off the flow of conversation or, in effect, "dragging" the speaker through the door, that is, forcing him or her to speak up. In this sense, such remarks become roadblocks to listening.

NONREFLECTIVE LISTENING MAY BE HELPFUL

Since many people are more inclined to talk than to listen, you would think there would be unlimited opportunity for nonreflective listening. In fact, people sometimes mistakenly stereotype all listening as nonreflective. But nonreflective listening is more appropriate in some situations than in others. It is sometimes difficult, however, to determine whether nonreflective listening is appropriate, because that depends mostly on the particular situation, the speaker, the listener, and the purpose of their communication. A general rule is that nonreflective listening is especially helpful whenever the speaker needs to ventilate intense emotions like anger or grief, or tell us something which requires only minimal response on our part. For example, nonreflective listening may be helpful in the following types of situations:

1. *The speaker is eager to tell us his or her particular attitude or viewpoint about something.* This is why so many psychotherapists readily engage in nonreflective listening at the outset of therapy. Before making any comments, a therapist wants to understand the client's problems, how they feel about them, and so forth. Consequently, it is not unusual to hear a client come back from a therapeu-

tic session, especially in the early part of a counseling relationship, saying things like "My therapist hardly said a thing, I did all the talking." Or, "I wasn't sure what to say, but I spent practically all the time talking."

Nonreflective listening is also appropriate in interviewing, especially in the "unstructured" interview in which an employer wants to learn as much as possible about someone. As the interviewer, you might initiate the conversation with an open question like "What part of your job do you enjoy the most?" or "Why do you want to work for us?" Then, as it seems appropriate, you may add occasional neutral responses as a way of facilitating the speaker's self-expression. Nonreflective listening to a person's viewpoint or explanation behind a proposal, complaint, or grievance is also useful. It is especially helpful for those in sales, service, and negotiations where more understanding is needed before a response is made. Otherwise, one tends to go off "half-cocked," making false assumptions, telling people things they do not want to hear, or answering questions they haven't raised.

2. *The speaker feels a need to ventilate intense feelings.* Here, nonreflective listening is just what the doctor orders. Otherwise, the speaker's pent-up emotions constantly interfere with any attempt to hold a rational, two-way conversation. When a person has a problem or complaint, that person will generally be anxious, fearful, disappointed, hurt, angry, or resentful. At such times, people need to "get something off their chests." A wise listener allows the person just to talk and express whatever emotion may come forth, with minimum responses. Nonreflective listening is most appropriate for this kind of pressure-cooker situation.

I learned the value of this early in my career. While in training as a psychotherapist, I was also working as an Assistant Dean of Students in the university where I was doing graduate work. The Dean often told me, "The important thing is to *let the students talk.* I don't care what *you* say." At the time, that sounded like cynical advice to a budding therapist concerned with helping people. Yet, in due time, I found there was a measure of truth in what he said. For time and again, I found that students in trouble had a need to express their pent-up emotions, to "explain" why they were having trouble. Just letting them talk it out gave them a kind of catharsis, or emotional relief. It also helped me to understand them better, to know why they were acting the way they were. When people are not allowed to talk, they sometimes come back with hostile remarks like "You're not listening to me," or "Just listen for a minute."

3. *The speaker has difficulty expressing his or her personal concerns or problems.* Here, nonreflective listening minimizes the interruptions, thereby facilitating self-expression. Even tape recorders and specially programed computers may do this. In one experiment, people were paid to talk into tape recorders about anything they pleased and then were paid different amounts depending on how much they talked, measured by a digital counter. Some talked every day, five days a week, for up to 300 sessions, comparable to the length of short psychoanalysis! Few missed a single session. Many felt better for having had the opportunity to talk, and a few even preferred the tape recorder to human listeners. Furthermore, when portions of the tapes were compared to geniune interpersonal interviews, it was difficult to tell which was which. Another experiment involved talking into a specially programed computer utilizing minimal responses. The subject sat down in front of a display screen with a typewriter keyboard attached. After some questions desinged to get name, address, age, sex, and other identifying information, the computer asked open-ended questions like "Is anything bothering you?" or "Have you been feeling sad?" If the speaker pushed the YES button, the computer screen then read "OK, the tape recorder is now running, you may talk about your feelings." When the subject began talking, the computer simply added "Good! We are listening to you talk about your feelings."

Only three of the thirty-two subjects answered NO to all thirteen questions regarding emotional problems. Of those who answered YES, twenty-two proceeded to discuss a problem with the computer. One of the most common problems was a feeling of sadness. Another frequent problem was that of self-expression. Almost half felt they had trouble expressing themselves. For these people, the machine gave minimal responses and clearly facilitated self-expression. People felt better. About a fourth of the people even felt more at ease talking to a computer than a human. While human listeners at their *best* were better than the computer, at their *worst* they made more mistakes—needless interruptions and judgmental remarks—all of which closed more doors than they opened.[2]

4. *The speaker may be inhibited talking to someone with greater authority, power, or status.* People often hesitate to speak up to their superiors for fear of jeopardizing their relationships or their jobs. As we said earlier, a lot depends on the particular situation, the speaker, the listener, and the purpose of their communication. But generally, people with greater authority or power feel freer to initiate conversations and interrupt more frequently, thereby dominating the conversation. In fact, interruptions are a way of asserting power. But the result is often one-way communication, with the more "powerful" people hearing what they want to hear rather than what they need to hear. Or as one executive put it, "yes men" are even more dangerous than those who constantly question and object to what we do.

Realizing how power affects communication adversely, anyone in a position of authority—whether a parent, teacher, therapist, public official, manager, or executive—can encourage better communication through a greater use of nonreflective listening. Appropriate nonreflective listening shows that you are interested, that you want to know other people's views and feelings, that you want to be informed—even of their criticism and complaints. Not surprisingly, one study showed that front-line supervisors of "high morale" workers were twice as likely to hear their complaints and grievances as those of "low morale" workers. It was not that the former supervisors were less interested in production; it was just that they were more "employee-oriented." Actually, their workers achieved higher production than those of the "production-oriented" supervisors![3]

[2] Charles W. Slack and Warner V. Slack, "Good! We are Listening to You Talk About Your Sadness," *Psychology Today*, January 1974, pp. 63–65.
[3] Research findings from the Institute for Social Research, University of Michigan, in Harry W. Hepner, *Psychology Applied to Life and Work* (5th ed.) Englewood Cliffs, N.J.: Prentice-Hall, Inc., 1973.

There are a variety of other situations in which nonreflective listening may be especially appropriate. Shy, nonassertive people often do better with patient, unobtrusive listeners. Long ago, I discovered that those who remain quiet in a class or group are not necessarily the least able members. Sometimes they are extremely able, they are simply more reticent to speak up in a group. Then too, people are sometimes attracted to their respective occupations because they are more comfortable with "things" than with people. People who work with figures, mechanical things, or in labs or research settings do not always have the necessary skills for expressing themselves readily in face-to-face relationships. Furthermore, people going through a crisis, like the loss of a job, the breakup of their marriage, or the death of a loved one, often need a "sounding board" more than advice. In times like these, nonreflective listening, sometimes accompanied by appropriate nonverbal communication like the touch of a hand, communicates understanding and acceptance more adequately than a lot of words.

WHEN NONREFLECTIVE LISTENING ISN'T ENOUGH

As valuable as nonreflective listening is, it can easily be misused. Sometimes inexperienced professional helpers may unconsciously avoid their responsibilities by doing too much nonreflective listening when a more active response is needed. Then too, we may easily kill off topics introduced by others by pausing a moment or so before uttering some kind of noncommittal response like "I guess so." Too many long pauses or too much silence tends to express disinterest or rejection, whether this is intentional or not. Furthermore, we are all familiar with the power of the "silent treatment," by which not only husbands and wives but coworkers avoid one another in uncharacteristic silence. Consequently, nonreflective listening may easily be misused or overdone. It is *not* likely to be appropriate in the following types of situations.

1. *The speaker is not sufficiently motivated or eager to talk to warrant our nonreflective listening.* Since one of the purposes of nonreflective

listening is to facilitate the speaker's self-expression, it presupposes a speaker who has "something to say." When the speaker has no pressing concern, no strong emotions, no real message to communicate, other than routine social talk, nonreflective listening is not only inappropriate but often impossible or rude.

This was brought home to me by a young woman in a class for parents. After working on listening skills in class, the young mother returned the next week a bit skeptical. "I tried to listen to my children," she said, "but they didn't have anything to say." She had made the common mistake of thinking others will be ready to talk when we are ready to listen. More often than not, it works the other way. People are eager to tell us something at *their* convenience, which may not be at *our* convenience. But it is then we need to listen. Later in the course, that same mother told of an incident in which her children were eager to talk and she had listened to them nonreflectively with gratifying results.

2. *The speaker mistakenly takes our nonreflective listening to mean we agree when we don't.* One of the dangers of listening is that people will misinterpret our empathy as sympathy, our understanding as agreement. Furthermore, this doesn't usually become apparent until some later occasion when we make our disagreement more explicit—sometimes days or weeks later. At that point, the speaker may express surprise and disappointment, saying something like "I thought you agreed." Attempts to explain that we listened as a way of expressing understanding rather than agreement are often taken to mean that we have either changed our mind, or even worse, are hypocrites. For this reason, when we listen to understand someone's views or feelings, while honestly disagreeing with what we hear, it is sometimes best to state this explicitly. Our feelings may interrupt the flow of conversation and even provoke an open disagreement. But not to do so runs a risk of even greater misunderstanding and resentment at some later date.

3. *Sometimes the speaker seeks a more active form of support or reassurance than afforded by nonreflective listening.* In these instances, the speaker not only wants to be understood but also may want active support, reassurance, or guidance. This is one reason why many

therapists shift to a more active involvement with their clients in the later stages of therapy. Once a person's problems and needs have been uncovered, something must be done about them, positive goals must be set, and growth experienced. All of this requires more active, two-way communication between therapist and client than in the beginning of therapy. Similarly, when people ask us for our reactions, views, or suggestions—whether they be adolescents, students, neighbors or customers—simply to respond with nonreflective listening will be perceived as a rejection. In these instances, it is usually more appropriate to use reflective, empathetic listening, along with more initiative in expressing our own views and reactions.

4. *Nonreflective listening is no longer appropriate when it thwarts our own needs for self-expression and evokes resentment toward the speaker.* For example, a woman who tried to listen to her talkative mother-in-law ended up resenting her all the more. The woman realized that her mother-in-law probably talked too much because she was lonely. So, on a long trip, the woman decided to listen to her mother-in-law as long as the latter wanted to talk. As it happened, the older woman talked without interruption throughout the entire trip. Early on, however, the daughter-in-law realized she was no longer listening to the older woman's endless chatter. Instead, she found herself resenting the older woman as a self-centered person who dominated others through constant talking. She also realized that martyrs do not make good listeners.

There is always the danger that nonreflective listening will be exploited by overly talkative people, especially those who are insensitive to the needs of others or those who try to control others through talking. One man I know prides himself on being able to handle long-winded people on the telephone. He does so by continuing to be busy with his hands, sometimes interrupting the speaker to speak to his secretary—in effect, not really listening. Furthermore, when he puts down the phone, he tends to make an uncomplimentary face as if to disparage the long-winded speaker. In these cases, it would be better if we told such a person tactfully, but firmly, "I am busy right now, can you get to the main point?" We are more likely to hear what is then said, and have a better attitude toward the speaker.

More than not, the advantages of nonreflective listening outweigh its disadvantages. But only experience and judgment will determine whether nonreflective listening will be appropriate for a given situation. When in doubt, you can refer back to the guidelines given in this chapter. When nonreflective listening isn't enough, you may want to use reflective listening, explained in the next chapter.

EXERCISES

USE OF MINIMAL RESPONSES.   Most of us use these neutral, door-opener responses without being fully aware of it. The purpose of this exercise is to become more aware of the differences between neutral, door-opener type responses that facilitate communication, and the more familiar roadblocks to listening.

Since reading this chapter, have you become aware of other people using these responses? How about yourself? Do you use some of them more than others? Which ones?

The next time someone initiates a conversation in which it is *appropriate,* try nonreflective listening. Throughout your listening, try to become more aware of your responses to the speaker. Which responses seem to come natural to you?

Did you make any responses which had a negative effect, that is, stopped the flow of conversation or made the speaker defensive? What were they?

When it seems appropriate, take your cue from someone's nonverbal communication, responding with door-openers such as "You look happy," "You look tired," and so forth. Notice the effect of your comment.

HELPING OTHERS TO VENTILATE INTENSE FEELINGS.   The next time your are confronted with someone under the spell of an intense emotion, try drawing that person out with nonreflective listening. It is usually easier dealing with feelings toward someone other than yourself. It is also easier listening to positive emotions such as love, joy, and admiration. Yet nonreflective listening is even more helpful to speakers expressing negative emotions like anxiety, fear, disappointment, hurt, jealousy, and anger.

When you are listening to someone expressing strong emotions, try to keep out of the speaker's way as much as possible. Avoid interrupting, or making judgmental responses, including "agreeing" or "sympathizing" responses—all roadblocks to listening. Did you feel nonreflective listening helped the other person express himself or herself? How satisfied did the speaker seem to feel after talking things out? Did the intensity of emotions decrease somewhat as the conversation proceeded? Did you learn something about this person's attitudes and feelings through nonreflective listening?

ENCOURAGING "LESS POWERFUL" PEOPLE TO SPEAK UP. The purpose of this exercise is to become more aware of how authority, power, and status affect our communication, especially in bringing about "one-way" communication with those of less authority or status than ourselves. Since reading the last two chapters, perhaps you have already become aware of how people with greater power tend to dominate a conversation by talking more or interrupting more frequently. How about yourself? Have you become aware of doing this in relation to those in positions with less authority than yourself? Or have you become more sensitive to people with greater authority who do this to you?

Either way, the next time someone with *less* authority or status than yourself initiates a conversation with you, try nonreflective listening as a way of deliberately encouraging that person to express himself or herself more freely. If you are a parent, try this with your children or adolescents. If you are the leader of a committee or group, try it out during a group meeting. Or if you are a supervisor, manager, or executive, try it out when you passively listen to someone in your office.

Did nonreflective listening help the other person to speak more freely? Did you gain a better understanding of this person's views or feelings through nonreflective listening? In which types of situations would it be helpful for you to practice nonreflective listening more regularly?

LISTENING TO COMPLAINTS AND GRIEVANCES.   This is the acid test of listening. It is also the time when we most need to listen. When people come to you with a complaint or grievance, they are usually talking about something which affects them personally, and about which they have strong emotions. More often than not, they have already experienced considerable frustration, if not rebuff, from others. At the same time, people often express themselves poorly, especially when they are emotionally aroused. As a result, they seem to be attacking us when they really aren't. In turn, we tend to become defensive, reacting emotionally, and listening poorly, if at all.

The next time someone airs a complaint or grievance to you, try drawing them out with nonreflective listening. This may work best when the complaint is directed at someone other than yourself. Obviously, nonreflective listening is even more helpful when the complaint or grievance is directed at you, but this is also more difficult. Either way, try to be accepting and try not to take what is said personally. Avoid defensive responses that stifle or distort the speaker's message. Remember, people often do not mean to attack you; it just comes out that way.

Did the speaker's emotions become somewhat less intense as the conversation proceeded? Did the speaker feel more satisfied at having the opportunity to talk things out without interruption? Through nonreflective listening, did you also learn something about the person's attitudes and viewpoint? Which minimal responses, if any, worked best for you in that situation?

CHAPTER FOUR

REFLECTIVE
LISTENING

When nonreflective listening is not enough, you may need to listen reflectively. Essentially, reflective listening is the process of giving nonjudgmental feedback to the speaker as a way of checking on the accuracy of what has been heard. Sometimes this is called "active" listening, because the listener is more actively verbalizing his or her understanding of the speaker's message than in nonreflective listening. Yet, as we said earlier, all listening, as opposed to hearing, is inherently an active process, though reflective listening is more obviously so. Reflective listening is also riskier than nonreflective listening, since we expose our understanding for criticism and correction. But more importantly, reflective listening helps us to achieve greater accuracy in communication.

Psychotherapists and others who are skilled in working with people have long practiced reflective listening to help their clients gain greater understanding of their feelings and problems. Now, people in practically all fields are discovering that reflective listening is necessary for accurate communication and more satisfying relationships.

The essentials of reflective listening appear deceptively simple on paper, but once you begin using them, you will discover that these skills are not so easily acquired. Initially, such skills may seem awkward to you. Usually, it takes considerable practice and experience before one can listen reflectively in an easy, natural manner. This is why most people never acquire the skills of reflec-

43

tive listening, which is to say most people never really learn to listen in the true sense of the word.

NEED FOR REFLECTIVE LISTENING

Reflective skills are necessary for good listening, mostly because of the difficulties inherent in the process of communication itself. Let's take a look at several of these limitations.

First, most words have more than one meaning. For the 500 most commonly used words in the English language, there are over 14,000 different meanings, or about twenty-eight meanings per word. Sometimes this makes it difficult to determine what someone means by a given word without knowing its particular connotation to the speaker. For example, how often have you asked someone "What do you mean by that?" Or possibly you have had to try answering such a question yourself. Most likely the speaker will try to get across his or her meaning in different words. This is because words are imprecise vehicles for conveying the personal meaning of speakers. Sometimes it is hard to find just the right word to say what you want to say. The reason is that the meaning is in the speaker's mind, not in the words themselves. As a result, reflective skills must be employed to check on the meaning of the words used.

Second, messages must be decoded for their meaning. That is, much of what we communicate is personally meaningful to ourselves, whether it be ideas, attitudes, feelings, or facts. When we attempt to communicate these meanings in socially acceptable ways, we tend to "code" them in socially acceptable ways. We choose our words carefully to avoid offending. We are subtle. We are circumspect, we are "cool." Because of this, we often fail to convey our meaning so the listener will really understand. Just as the military establishment conceals its messages in codes for reasons of national security, individuals also wrap their personal messages in codes for reasons of personal security. As a result, the listener must give feedback in order to decode the coded message and get the personal meanings conveyed. See the illustration on the next page.

Intended message	Coded message	Perceived meaning
Everyone has to work harder to get the new job done on time.	I want to see you really sweat these next few weeks.	(Inaccurate decoding) The boss has it in for me. (Accurate decoding) All of us have to work harder.

Third, people have difficulty expressing themselves assertively. That is, because of social tact and the need for approval, people often begin a request or reaction with mild prefaces that are not clear in their intent. Those who show up in a therapist's office usually begin with one or more "presenting" problems, few of which are the main concern. Only as clients feel safe and accepted do they express their deeper problems. Often such issues emerge only toward the end of a session, when time does not permit further discussion.

People do much the same thing in everyday conversation. That is, they test the water before diving into the more emotionally loaded topics. The less assertive people are, the more they "beat around the bush" before getting to the main point. consequently, we need to listen reflectively in order to understand what people are getting at.

Finally, subjective factors also contaminate communication. People may be blinded by their attitudes, emotions, or past training and experience. In other words, each of us has grown up and worked in different settings with different people. All of this has socialized us to affirm certain behaviors and condemn or shun others. It also serves to code our messages in personal ways as a speaker, and to filter out certain things as a listener.

All this points to the need for reflective listening skills to decode messages for their intended meaning. Throughout the rest of this chapter we will explain four types of reflective responses: clarifying, paraphrasing, reflecting feelings, and summarizing. Ordinarily, these skills are used in combination, but we will discuss them separately for the purpose of explanation.

45

CLARIFYING

These are responses asking the speaker for clarification. Clarifying responses help the speaker make his or her message more readily understandable, thus facilitating a more accurate reception on the listener's part. To get additional facts or meanings, as a listener you might say something like. "Would you please clarify that?" Or when you want to see more of the problem as a whole, you might say "Is this the problem as you see it?" Such responses encourage the speaker to elaborate or clarify the original message in a way that helps the listener better understand what is being said. While there is no one right way to phrase clarifying responses, the following "openers" may be useful:

> "Would you say that again?"
> "I don't understand what you mean."
> "Would you clarify that?"
> "I don't get it."
> "What do you mean?"
> "Would you translate that?"

Some of these openers are simple declarative statements which serve the purpose of making the speaker *aware* you do not fully understand what is being said. Frequently, such a remark is all that is needed because speakers usually do not realize they are not making themselves clear. Such a simple reminder on the listener's part may encourage the speaker to make greater efforts at communicating more clearly. Note that these remarks focus on the speaker's message or the process of communication itself, rather than on the speaker's personality. Listeners want to encourage the speaker to *do* something more, to *communicate* more clearly. When you imply there is something wrong with the speaker, he or she becomes defensive, thereby making it more difficult to communicate clearly.

You will also note that several of these clarifying responses are "open" questions. That is, they simply encourage speakers to enlarge or elaborate on their original communication. You can also use "closed" questions for this purpose, those which call for a simple yes or no response. Examples include responses such as "Is that the problem?" "Would you prefer to do it yourself?" and "Is that all you wanted to say?" Yet closed questions should be used sparingly for several reasons. First, they tend to disrupt the speaker's train of thought. Have you ever felt cut off in a conversation by such a question? Second, such questions quickly switch the focus of the communication from the speaker to the listener. Unwittingly, the listener controls the conversation in this manner, quickly putting the speaker on the defensive. Consequently, open questions or responses are usually preferable. Simple declarative statements such as "I don't understand what you mean," are best because the listener indicates his willingness to remain neutral until the full message is accurately conveyed.

In the following example, what seems a paradox at first becomes clear only through the listener's patient skill at asking for clarification.

Jim: Despite poor sales last year, we are all getting higher quotas for next year.

Ann: How's that again?

Jim: Even though most of us didn't reach last year's sales quotas, we are getting higher ones this year because our territories are being split up differently.

Ann: Could you explain that a little more?

Jim: I mean, the company has decided to have fewer, but larger territories for each sales rep. That's why each of us will have a higher sales quota next year, regardless of what we sold last year.

Ann: Oh, I see.

Rather than react emotionally, Ann used clarifying skills to straighten out the speaker's message until it made sense to her.

PARAPHRASING

Paraphrasing responses consist of "restating" or "reflecting" meaning. Whatever we choose to call it, the skill of paraphrasing consists of serving back the gist of the speaker's message in the listener's own words. The listener who attempts to paraphrase a speaker's message is gambling, in a sense, that he or she has indeed heard the message correctly. No one wishes to have a *mis*understanding exposed. On the other hand, the greater accuracy of understanding that is achieved makes paraphrasing worthwhile.

The purpose of paraphrasing is to restate the speaker's message as a way of checking on its accuracy. In this sense, paraphrasing goes a step beyond the clarifying response. When we are unclear what the speaker is saying, we are more likely to ask for clarification. When we think we understand what the speaker is saying, however, then it is more appropriate to paraphrase the speaker's message.

To give some examples, paraphrasing responses often begin with phrases like:

"As I understand you . . ."
"You mean . . ."
"What I hear you saying is . . ."
"From your point of view . . ."
"You think . . ."
"Correct me if I am wrong, but . . ."
"In other words, your view is . . ."

In paraphrasing it is important that you attempt to capture only the essence or main points of the speaker's message. Otherwise, your response will only serve to confuse, rather than confirm the message. In this sense, paraphrasing consists in *selective*, rather than exhaustive repetition of what is said. Of course, in doing this you risk missing the main point, but this is precisely what paraphrasing is all about, that is, expressing your understanding of the speaker's message to find out how accurate it is.

Paraphrasing should also focus on the *content* of what is said, rather than the feelings expressed, though this is a relative distinction. In paraphrasing, we are primarily concerned with meanings and ideas rather than attitudes and feelings.

It is also very important for listeners to paraphrase in their own words. Otherwise, one would be falling into the error of "parroting," or woodenly repeating exact words. This practice of mirroring back someone's exact words, sometimes encountered among mentally disturbed people, serves to stifle the conversation. It also serves to baffle the speaker, who may wonder if he or she has really been heard. Paraphrasing the speaker's message in our own words, however, lets the speaker know we heard and understood what has been said. If not, we are asking to be corrected.

An illustration: A new woman employee in a bank has been assigned the drive-in window. When there are no customers at the window, she is supposed to help at the inside counters as well. If a customer shows up at the drive-in window, the first available teller is supposed to take it. But this almost never happens. The new employee expresses some resentment about the lack of cooperation, and her manager paraphrases:

Marie: "I am busier than the other tellers. I help at the inside counters as I am supposed to, but if a customer comes to the drive-in window, none of the other tellers help out. It is not fair."

Manager: "In other words, you are doing more than your share."

Marie: "That is right."

REFLECTING FEELINGS

Here, the listener reflects or mirrors back to the speaker the *feelings* being expressed. The focus is on the speaker's feelings, attitudes, or emotional reactions rather than on the content of the message as in paraphrasing. As we mentioned earlier, the distinction between the feelings and the content of our communication is somewhat arbitrary and not always easy to discern, but it is often a crucial one. Just think for a moment how satisfying it is when you feel strongly about something and someone picks up your feelings rather than getting hung up on the content which is only secondary to your "message."

For example, on the first day of our family vacation we had

planned to drive all day and have dinner that evening with old friends. After half a day's travel and considerable frustration, however, we had to return home and put the car in the shop for repairs. I reluctantly called our host to apologize and give all the reasons why we would not be able to make it for dinner. Being an experienced psychiatrist, our friend responded to my feelings, saying, "You have had a frustrating day!" At first, I was taken aback by his response, thinking "He is treating me like a client." Then, rather suddenly, I heaved a sigh of relief. He understood. His sharing of my feelings of frustration at that moment was far more important to me than getting across all the details of why we would not be there for dinner.

This experience points out another purpose of reflecting feelings, that is, to help the speaker discover his or her emotions more fully. We grow up in a society that has taught us to overcontrol our feelings, with the result that we often lose touch with our emotions and have difficulty expressing them. Consequently, hearing our feelings mirrored back to us can help us discover what we are feeling at the moment. For example, in the above illustration, I was so busy making all the necessary readjustments because of car trouble, that I had not been fully aware of how frustrated I was. My friend's response helped to make me more aware of my feelings, which in turn helped me face the situation more realistically, rather than strike out irrationally and become even more frustrated.

It is important to respond to people's feelings because communication is essentially people communicating with people about things which are personally meaningful to them. Consequently, much communication consists of feelings, attitudes, and emotional reactions—things which are highly meaningful to people—as well as factual information. All of this points to the wisdom in an old eastern proverb which goes "Listen to what people *say*, but find out how they *feel*."

Since the purpose of reflecting feelings is to let the speaker know we understand how he or she feels, our responses should be phrased in our own words as much as possible. Yet there are some opening phrases which can serve to facilitate a reflective response to feelings, such as:

"You feel . . ."
"You appear to be feeling . . ."
"Perhaps you are feeling . . ."
"Do you feel a little . . ."
"You are (sad, angry, etc.) . . ."
"It appears that you feel . . ."
"Maybe you feel . . ."
"I somehow sense that you feel . . ."
"You are feeling a bit . . ."

When the speaker's emotions become more intense, your response can fit the intensity expressed by the simple addition of the appropriate adverb:

"You feel *somewhat* frustrated."
"You feel *quite* frustrated."
"You feel *very* frustrated."
"You feel *extremely* frustrated."

There are several ways of recognizing feelings. First, watch for feeling words such as sad, angry, happy, and so forth. These are the main clues for identifying the feelings being expressed. Second, look for the nonverbal clues, such as facial expressions, tone of voice, posture, hand gestures, and spatial distance (that is, whether the speaker stands back or moves up close). Third, think of what you would be feeling if you were in the speaker's shoes. And finally, try to identify the overall context of communication, including the reasons why the speaker is talking to you. This often helps you to recognize the emotions being expressed.

Many times, of course, people express their feelings in a less direct, somewhat disguised fashion, especially when judging or criticizing others. For example, returning to my vacation illustration again, suppose I had launched into a tirade about how they were not making cars the way they used to, and how much repairs cost these days. It would have been much more difficult for my friend to have picked up my feelings of frustration. A less experienced listener could have easily become distracted by all the content details, such that we would have gotten into a meaningless discussion of automobiles, rather than my feelings of frustration, which was the main message.

SUMMARIZING

Summarizing responses sum up the main ideas and feelings expressed by the speaker in the conversation as a whole. This is more appropriate in larger segments of a conversation than were covered in the discussion of paraphrasing or reflecting feelings. For example, summarizing statements help to tie together the fragments of a conversation into a meaningful whole. They may help you as the listener to be certain you have accurately heard the "message" of the speaker, and may also help the speaker to know he or she has communicated well. Otherwise, you may walk away from a conversation not sure if you have heard the other's message. And the speaker, in turn, may be uncertain whether his or her message has been communicated.

As with the other responses described so far, it is best to put summary statements into your own words. But some typical opening comments for summary statements are:

"What you have said so far is . . ."
"Your key ideas, as I get it, are . . ."
"Everything you have said so far . . ."
"Now, summing up . . ."
"Recapping what you have been saying . . ."

For example, suppose a long and loyal customer has come to complain about your company's service as follows:

Mr. Brown: Two out of the last six shipments have come over a week late. Each time that cost us over $1,000 a day. Also, the last time we ordered parts from you, they were late. That's never happened before. Even the service has been less effective lately. What's happening around here?

Manager: You feel that we are letting you down all around—

shipments, parts, and now the service. And you want
to know what the story is, right?

Mr. Brown: Right.

Summarizing is especially appropriate in situations involving a discussion of differences, conflicts, complaints, or in which some type of problem solving is required. It is also helpful in groups and committee meetings in which the prolonged discussion of a subject may become unduly complicated, if not confusing. Without summary statements, the group may spend its energy reacting to surface manifestations of a problem rather than the basic issue or problem itself. Summarizing is also useful at the close of a telephone conversation, especially when several points have been covered, or something is to be done by the listener.

LEARNING TO LISTEN REFLECTIVELY

Invariably, when people are just beginning to listen reflectively, they say it feels awkward and artificial. Typical reactions are: "It's not spontaneous." "It's not me." What people fail to realize is that we must always pass through such a self-conscious stage in learning a new skill, whether it be driving, dancing, or listening. Perhaps reflective listening seems a bit more awkward because it involves modifying the way we deal with people. But it is the same process.

Someone has described four stages in learning to listen reflectively, as illustrated below.[1]

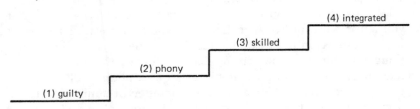

---

[1] From Dr. Thomas Gordon's *Instructor's Training Manual.* Copyright 1972 Effectiveness Training, Inc., Solana Beach, CA 92075. Used by permission.

As people become more conscious of their habitual tendency to judge, interpret, and interrupt others, they initially (1) feel guilty about this because of their new awareness of listening. Then, as they begin to practice reflective listening, (2) such skills may not only seem new, but phony to them. They become highly self-conscious, feeling they are manipulating others. As they acquire more experience in listening, however, they (3) begin to feel more skilled at listening reflectively. Finally, they acquire self-confidence and ease in using these skills, and (4) integrate them into their overall repertoire of communication skills in a way that feels natural to them.

There is no necessary time requirement for passing through these four stages. It is a matter of practice and experience. But most people take several weeks or months in reaching the third stage, depending on whether they have access to supervision, workshops, or jobs in which they get daily practice in their listening skills.

A final matter concerns your response as a listener when the speaker has requested some sort of action. As important as it is to express an accurate understanding of the speaker's request verbally, it is even more important that you demonstrate an appropriate action response. This has been referred to as "closing the loop" of listening by doing something tangible to show that you've genuinely "heard" the speaker's message. This is especially important in the areas of marketing, sales, and service where the speakers are clients or customers. Too often, a listener will say something such as "I will get back to you on this." But when nothing happens after weeks or months, the speaker may wonder, and rightfully so, if she or he was really heard.

Closing the loop of listening doesn't necessarily mean that you agree with the speaker. This is a common misunderstanding we will discuss in the next chapter. But it does mean doing something tangible to demonstrate that you heard the speaker. This may involve something as simple as a quick phone call to pursue the speaker's request or a written reminder of something to be done at a later date. As Thomas Carlyle once observed, "Doubt of any sort cannot be removed except by action."

Interestingly enough, one corporation asked its marketing

department to find out how its investors, customers, and prospects perceived the company. They found one of the things that kept coming up in customer remarks was that people in this company "really listened to you." Encouraged by this survey, the company launched a several million dollar campaign to further develop better listening among its employees. Several thousand managers have been trained to listen more effectively. Even the secretarial personnel in the sales and service divisions are being trained in listening as a way of better showing the customers that this company "cares." The corporation wisely avoided making questionable claims like "We listen better." Instead, they have adopted a believable slogan, "We Understand How Important it is to Listen," which serves as an expression of management philosophy at every level of the company.[2]

EXERCISES

CLARIFYING RESPONSES.   Perhaps you know people at work or at home who have difficulty making themselves clear. The next time such a person has something to tell you, try drawing them out with the aid of a clarifying response. Did you find that this helped the person to communicate with you more effectively? Did you find it more satisfying, helping you to understand this person better?

Clarifying responses can be used to great advantage in all sorts of communication. But it is especially helpful in trying to understand complicated situations, emotionally laden topics, or to follow an issue being discussed in a group. All too frequently, committee meetings get "bogged down," and a long series of verbal exchanges between several members becomes increasingly confusing to everyone involved, until someone comes to the rescue seeking clarification.

Whenever it is appropriate to do so, apply your clarifying skills at meetings in which you participate. Try to notice the result. Did it help? How?

[2] *Listening: The First Year.* Sperry Corporation, 1980.

PARAPHRASING RESPONSES. Do the same exercise as above, using paraphrasing responses. Remember that your purpose is to let the speaker know that you accurately understood what was said. Do not judge, analyze, or add to the speaker's message. Simply try to capture the gist of the message accurately in your own words.

Ask someone to role-play this exercise with you. Make certain the speaker selects a real issue of genuine concern to him or her. Otherwise, this could turn out to be an empty exercise in words. It should also be something he or she feels relatively safe discussing. Try paraphrasing the speaker's message for five or ten minutes at the most. Then ask the speaker how well you have understood what was said.

Did you find this was more difficult to do than you thought? Most people do. This exercise is even more meaningful when the partners switch roles.

REFLECTING FEELINGS. Take an 8½" x 11" sheet of paper and make two headings on it as shown below. Then for each example in the left-hand column, write a single word or short phrase in the answer column that sums up the feeling being expressed. Ask yourself "What is the speaker trying to tell me?"

Speaker says	*Feelings expressed*
a. I've had it up to here with your excuses.	
b. Okay, I apologized. What more do you want me to do?	
c. I couldn't do another paper at this point if I tried.	
d. You want to check my answer?	
e. I shouldn't have treated her that way.	
f. Can't you wait until after the weekend to take up our projects? I've got another test on Friday too.	

Speaker says	*Feelings expressed*

g. He seems to do everything well, even though he hasn't had as much experience as I have.

h. I can't figure those people out. Maybe we should stop trying to satisfy them.

i. I'll never help her again, not a single word of thanks for all that I did for her.

j. We could try it again, but frankly I don't think it's worth it.

After you have completed the right-hand column, compare your answers with the suggested ones below. Give yourself credit if you captured the main feeling message, whether you used exactly the same words or not. What percentage of the messages did you perceive accurately?

a. exasperated, wants results

b. feels enough has been said

c. feels worn out, exhausted

d. unsure of self, wants assurance

e. feels regret, guilt

f. pressured for time, overloaded

g. admiration, envy

h. feels discouraged, like quitting

i. bitter, resentful

j. skeptical, doubtful[3]

SUMMARIZING RESPONSES. A good time to practice this skill is the next time someone is discussing a rather complicated topic with you. Remember that summarizing is especially appropriate in situations involving a discussion of differences, conflicts, or in which some type of problem-solving is required.

If you are the leader or secretary of a committee, it may be

[3] Adapted from Dr. Thomas Gordon's participant notebook *Human Effectiveness Training*. Copyright 1972 Effectiveness Training, Inc., Solana Beach, CA 92075. Used by permission.

helpful to make summary statements toward the end of the meeting. Such statements not only check on the accuracy of what has been said throughout the meeting, but also help members to recall it better. This is especially helpful for those members who are expected to perform some further action before the next meeting. Even if you are not the secretary or leader of your group, take brief notes in the next meeting you attend and afterwards check them for accuracy with the person who conducted the meeting.

Note-taking during telephone calls also helps you to make good summarizing statements at the close of the conversation, especially when several points have been covered. if the message has to be transmitted to someone else, it is doubly helpful to check on its accuracy through point-by-point summarization.

THE LISTENING RULE.   A good way of practicing your reflective listening skills is the following exercise. The next time you are involved in a disagreement with someone, simply institute this rule. Each person is to speak only *after* restating the other person's ideas or feelings accurately, and to that person's satisfaction.

You will probably find this exercise is surprisingly difficult to do. Furthermore, you will also discover that each person is unconsciously using many of the roadblocks to listening discussed in the opening chapter. On the positive side, you may also experience a new level of understanding with another person. It is a relief to get feedback that says "I hear and understand you."

CHAPTER FIVE

ATTITUDE IS IMPORTANT

A major hazard in improving your listening habits is becoming preoccupied with the techniques of listening at the expense of the proper attitudes for listening. This is especially likely in the early stages of learning to listen reflectively, when people come across as a bit awkward and stilted. Even beginning counselors and therapists sometimes fall into this trap. Carl Rogers, who has trained thousands of professional therapists, has warned of the danger of confusing the empathetic attitude, which is so essential for listening, with a "wooden technique" of simply repeating back everything a client says.[1]

Attitude—our mental and emotional set toward a person or thing—is all-important in listening. When you have a positive attitude toward someone, you remain open and receptive to that person despite differences between you. But when you have a negative attitude toward someone, you become closed and unduly critical no matter how hard you try to listen. Negative attitudes can be even more detrimental to communication than faulty listening habits. This is why effective listening depends as much on positive attitudes as specific listening techniques. Leonard Sayles and George Strauss have expressed this point very well in their book *Managing Human Resources.*[2]

[1] Carl R. Rogers and Barry Stevens, *Person to Person* (Lafayette, CA: Real People Press, 1971), p. 90.

[2] Leonard R. Sayles and George Strauss, *Managing Human Resources* (2nd edition) (Englewood Cliffs, N.J.: Prentice-Hall, Inc., 1981), p. 114.

The listening approach is not something to be applied only when dealing with specific problems. It is a general attitude which the manager can apply day in and day out in dealings with fellow supervisors, subordinates, and the boss. In a nutshell, it is a matter of always being ready to listen to the other person's point of view and trying to take it into account before taking action oneself.

The three attitudes most essential for good listening are acceptance, self-acceptance, and empathy. While we will discuss each of these attitudes separately for the purpose of explanation, it is often best to combine them as an integral part of effective listening.

ACCEPTANCE

Acceptance, as it is used here, refers to more than a simple agreement, as in "accepting" the charges for a collect telephone call. Acceptance means a basic attitude of positive regard toward another person. In helping relationships, like counseling, acceptance has therapeutic powers in putting troubled people at ease, so they can express themselves and experience *self*-acceptance, too. Acceptance is no less essential in creating a favorable climate for communication in all human relationships, whether in the home, at the marketplace, or in the office.

The heart of acceptance is a nonjudgmental attitude. In many ways, this is just the opposite of the critical, judgmental attitude we so often exhibit in everyday relationships, as discussed in earlier chapters. Showing acceptance toward someone does not necessarily mean we agree with or approve of what that person says or does. Far from it. It simply means acknowledging that person's right to feel and think and act as he or she does, no matter how absurd these expressions may be. It implies our willingness to hear the person out. Acceptance means that we trust what others say is worthwhile, and that it will be adequately expressed. When we accept others, we hesitate to interrupt them, or "to put words into their mouth."

Acceptance also involves the positive valuing of another, as a person, with infinite worth and dignity. It implies that others have the right to their own views and their own lives, no matter how much they may differ from our own. Acceptance says to a person "You are able to make your own decisions and be responsible for your own life." Even though we may become deeply concerned about something another person is doing, acceptance leads us to express our concern in a way that others can take or leave what we say. Ordinarily, acceptance is accompanied by feelings of liking and warmth toward others, expressed in all kinds of subtle ways, like the warmth in our smile or voice. But it is also possible to be accepting of others without the presence of such feelings. In fact, acceptance is even more essential for good communication with those we *don't* like, especially in listening to complaints and criticisms.

An accepting attitude on the part of a listener puts the speaker at ease, instead of on the defensive, as is the case with critical, judgmental listeners. Speakers feel comfortable enough to think out what they want to say and to express it freely. Ironically, the less we judge speakers, the more apt they are to become self-critical, expressing their thoughts and feelings even more honestly than if they feel under scrutiny. Yet it is important that our acceptance be real, that it represent out inner attitude. Faking acceptance may make speakers feel even more uncomfortable than an honest admission of our biases toward them or what they say. Again, when it comes to communication, attitude is even more important than technique.

At this point, it is important to realize that none of us is perfectly accepting. Even though psychotherapists speak of the need for "unconditional acceptance" of their clients, this remains more of an ideal than an achievement in therapy, much less in everyday communication. The truth is, few people are consistently accepting of anyone all the time. Even close friends, lovers, and spouses vary in their day-to-day acceptance of each other. Some people, however, are generally more accepting of others because of their favorable past development and personality. But most of us tend to favor some people more than others. Then too, the level of our acceptance of another person is constantly shifting, depending on our needs and feelings, changes in others, and specific situations. In short, we aim at being as accepting as possible, realizing that no one is totally accepting.

SELF-ACCEPTANCE

Probably the single most important reason people have trouble accepting others is that they do not fully accept themselves. It is a well-known axiom in clinical practice that the less we have come to terms with something in ourselves, the less accepting we will be of this in others. For example, a perfectionistic person, who cannot tolerate her own inadequacies, will have difficulty accepting even the ordinary mistakes that everyone commits at one time or another, such as forgetting a meeting. Rather than listening to explanations that may yield helpful clues for preventing future occurrences, such a person may react with a tirade of disparaging comments about the other person's incompetency or stupidity, which only aggravates the situation.

By the same token, and looking on the positive side, the more we come to terms with ourselves, the more fully we can accept others. Here, again, acceptance does not mean blanket approval or resignation to our shortcomings, as much as a realistic acknowledgement that this is the way we are without being overjudgmental. It means being able to affirm ourselves as worthwhile persons, even while we are in the process of working on certain faults. Acknowledging our own inadequacies, fears, and failures, we can deal with those of others more rationally and helpfully. And since no one is perfectly self-accepting, it is usually a matter of degree.

The following profile, based on clinical experience and research, is characteristic of those with optimal self-acceptance. Read and consider them carefully to see how well you accept yourself.

1. They hold to their values and principles in the face of adverse group opinion, although they are secure enough to change when in error.
2. They are capable of acting on their own best judgment without feeling excessive guilt or regret if disapproved of by others.
3. They do not spend undue time worrying about tomorrow or yesterday.

4. They retain confidence in their ability to deal with problems, despite occasional failures and setbacks.
5. They feel equally worthwhile to others as persons, neither superior nor inferior because of differences in ability or position.
6. They are relatively relaxed in the presence of others, with an "I'm OK, you're OK" attitude.
7. They can accept compliments and praise without false modesty.
8. They tend to resist being dominated by others.
9. They are able to accept a wide range of feelings within themselves and others, without the compulsion to act on every feeling.
10. They are able to enjoy themselves in a wide variety of activities involving work, play, companionship, creative self-expression, or loafing.
11. They are sensitive to the needs of others, including accepted social customs.
12. They tend to look for the best in others, believing most people are pretty decent despite their shortcomings.[3]

The difference self-acceptance and acceptance make in listening may be seen in the following example. Jack, an experienced department manager whose years of working with people in stressful situations made him an asset to his company, was approached by Bill, a junior analyst. "Where in blazes is my binder? Nothing is ever where it belongs around here. Why don't you do something about it?"

Together they found the missing binder, without a word from the manager. Bill went back to work feeling ashamed of his angry tirade, and did not speak to Jack until the following day when he saw Jack putting a new book rack in the work area. Glancing at Bill, Jack said "How's that for your binders?" Flabbergasted, Bill said, "Gee, boss, I'm sorry I lashed out at you the other day. Afterwards I felt so guilty, especially when you didn't say anything. I just couldn't get it off my mind. Aren't you *mad* at me?" "You had a legitimate gripe, Bill," said Jack, "and of course I'm not mad. What good would that do? I've *been* mad at you and others,

[3] From *Encounters With the Self,* Second Edition, by Don E. Hamachek. Copyright © 1978 by Holt, Rinehart and Winston. Copyright © 1971 by Holt, Rinehart and Winston, Inc. Reprinted by permission of Holt, Rinehart and Winston.

but anger passes. We get over it and learn something in the process."

Jack's quiet self-assurance helped Bill to come to terms with his own anger. Because Jack had already experienced his own capacity for anger and accepted it, he was able to listen more effectively when Bill became angry.

EMPATHY

This is the third attitude essential for good communication. Empathy is being aware of another's feelings of anger, sorrow, joy, or what have you, and communicating that understanding to the other person.

Empathy is to be distinguished from both apathy and sympathy. *Apathy* (without feeling) is more likely to occur when we feel uninterested and uninvolved. With the constant bombardment by the mass media on the ills of others, a certain degree of detachment and selective apathy may be necessary for personal survival in our modern society. Yet apathy thwarts communication in the sense that people may become callous to the feelings of others and become overly concerned with efficiency, power, money, and status. *Sympathy* (feeling "for" another) is at the opposite extreme. We are more likely to feel sympathy when we are overinvolved with someone, whether a close friend, family member, neighbor, or a colleague at work. When we are feeling down, we may also seek out a friend with a "sympathetic ear." Yet sympathy can easily degenerate into an unhealthy overidentification with another, with an uncritical acceptance of someone's problems. A troubled person can become even more troubled in the company of those who sympathize to the extent of agreeing uncritically. Weak, overly sympathetic parents tend to spoil their children.

Empathy (feeling "with" or "into" another) refers to the awareness of a person's feelings, together with a vicarious affective response to that person. When we are empathetic toward someone, we understand that person's feelings within his or her own internal frame of reference. We want to know what their feelings mean to them, so we can understand them. We feel a person's feelings "as if" they were our own feelings. This "as if" quality is the key to empathy, in that empathy connotes sensitivity to others without a loss of our own identity and feelings. A spoken response out of empathy is the mark of a good listener.

Kenneth Clark points out that empathy is the very opposite of the egocentric insensitivity so common in everyday life. In their efforts at personal survival, humans tend to give priority to their own needs. They aspire to power as a way of insuring the gratification of their own needs, often becoming insensitive to others along the way. In contrast, empathy helps balance self-interest with the concern for others. It makes us social beings. Those completely lacking empathy, like the psychopath, remain overly preoccupied with the immediate gratification of their own needs and callous to the needs and hurts of others. On the other hand, those who become excessively empathetic, like the social reformer and saint, run the risk of jeopardizing their own survival by becoming overburdened with the problems of others. Most of us fall somewhere in between these two extremes, balancing self-gratification with empathy in varying degrees. Although we would probably call ourselves "realistic," we run the risk of having too little, rather than too much empathy.[4]

EMPATHETIC LISTENING

As the name implies, empathetic listening is communicating empathy through the ways we listen. We do this primarily through the various reflective listening skills discussed in Chapter 4, that is, through clarifying, paraphrasing, reflecting, and summarizing responses. For example, instead of saying "I feel empathy for you" to someone expressing his or her feelings of hurt over a recent divorce, you *demonstrate* your empathy by reflecting and restating: "You feel deeply hurt by your divorce."

Empathetic listening differs from active, reflective listening more in intent than in technique. That is, you will do many of the same things in both types of listening, such as being attentive and reflecting feelings. The basic difference lies in your aim or

[4] Kenneth B. Clark, "Empathy," *American Psychologist,* 1980, 35, 2, 187–190.

intention. In active, reflective listening, your aim is to hear the speaker's message as accurately as possible, whether ideas or deeply felt meanings. The aim of empathetic listening, on the other hand, is to pick up the *feeling* tone of those ideas and meanings from the other person's viewpoint. It involves getting inside his or her frame of reference and discovering what those expressed views mean and how that person feels about it. Ordinarily, empathetic listening implies an even more personal type of communication than does active listening.

Empathetic listening is just the opposite from critical, judgmental listening, with varying mixtures of the two extremes lying somewhere in between. For instance, think of the possible listener responses to someone who says "Every time I propose a new idea around here, it's shot down, so why try?"

An uncaring or insensitive listener might respond by saying something like "So why *don't* you stop trying?" or "I wouldn't worry about it as long as you keep your job." A more understanding listener might respond by saying "You are just tired of trying." An even more understanding empathetic listener would say something like "It is demoralizing to have all your ideas ignored" or "You are so discouraged you feel like giving up—but the thought of that bothers you."

You can readily see how empathetic listening produces a more positive response than judgmental listening. Instead of feeling ignored or judged (as in the first listener's response), the speaker is more likely to feel understood in a way that will encourage further expression of his or her feelings. As Carl Rogers says, "When someone understands how it feels and seems to be me without wanting to analyze or judge me, then I can blossom and grow up in that climate."[5] You can also see that empathetic listening is even more difficult to do than active listening. It requires an attitude of empathy as well as reflective techniques. Empathy means really wanting to understand another person, despite our fears of being criticized or changed by what we hear. Empathetic listening is especially needed in situations of high emotional involvement, such as personal conflicts, problem solving, and negotiations.

[5] Rogers and Stevens, *Person to Person,* p. 90.

SEX DIFFERENCES. What about the old cliché that women listen more empathetically than men? Perhaps you have heard this notion, so you won't be surprised to learn that there is some support for it.

According to the literature on sex differences in empathy, a lot depends on which aspect of empathy we mean. As regards mental awareness, or recognition of others' feelings in communication, as detected in facial expressions, men and women do equally well. It is only in the affective response to another's feelings, or the vicarious expression of those feelings, that women tend to excel. Put more succinctly, although men and women do equally well in recognizing other people's feelings, women tend to be more adept in expressing that awareness back to the other person empathetically. Since it is the speaker's *perception* of empathy that counts for so much, we can readily see why women listeners often seem more empathetic than men.[6] This was brought out in a study of management styles among men and women. Compared to men, women managers were perceived to be more concerned and attentive, gave out more information about their departments, were more receptive to subordinates' ideas, and were more encouraging of subordinates' efforts.[7]

The explanation for women's greater empathetic skill lies largely in the ways women and men are socialized. Men, in accordance with the male sex role, are taught to emphasize active mastery of their environment, including the ability to control their feelings. Women, on the other hand, are brought up with an emphasis on close, nurturing relationships, in which they can express their feelings more freely. They also learn to imagine themselves in another person's place, and to communicate effective responses back. The point here is that women's superior ability to communicate empathy is mostly learned.

Now that many women are taking assertiveness training to outgrow the shortcomings of a stereotyped female sex role, perhaps

[6] Martin L. Hoffman, "Sex Differences in Empathy and Related Behaviors," *Psychological Bulletin*, 1977, 84, 4, 712–722.

[7] John E. Baird and Patricia Hayes Bradley, "Styles of Management and Communication: A Comparative Study of Men and Women." *Communication Monographs*, June 1979, 101–111.

men could benefit from some sort of empathy training. The sensitivity training groups, so popular in the 1960s, were a step in that direction, in that many participants increased their ability to experience and express feelings of empathy toward others.[8] Also, men who work in the nurturant professions—psychiatrists, psychologists, social workers, and others—are equally adept at expressing their feelings of empathy, providing further evidence that empathy can be learned.[9]

THE IMPORTANCE OF EMPATHETIC LISTENING. It is hard to overestimate the importance of empathetic listening in creating the climate for effective communication. In addition to its effectiveness in therapeutic communication, empathy has also been found to be a key ingredient for success in many other occupations heavily dependent on communication and interpersonal relationships, like teaching, sales, and management.[10] Furthermore, as Carl Rogers points out, even the desire to empathize may be helpful. That is, just the *attitude* of wanting to understand someone is valuable in and of itself.[11] Interestingly enough, even though psychotherapists list empathy as the most important quality of an ideal therapist, recordings of these same therapists have shown that many of them fall short of their ideal, which reminds us that an empathetic attitude is no easy achievement.[12]

Empathetic listening is especially valuable in the face of differences and conflicts. Our willingness to listen empathetically to those we disagree with may help to preserve communication. For example, if someone is explaining his or her work or giving a report and you must disagree, listen carefully to the person's reasoning first, and then respond to it, pointing out how your own view differs. If you restate that person's viewpoint in your own words before giving your own, you lessen the risk that your opinion will be taken

[8] Marvin D. Dunnette, "People Feeling: Joy, More Joy, and the 'Slough of Despond.'" *Journal of Applied Behavioral Science*, 1969, 5, 25–44.

[9] R. Rosenthal, et al. "Body Talk and Tone of Voice: The Language Without Words," *Psychology Today*, September 1974, pp. 64–68.

[10] D. N. Aspy, "Empathy," *The Counseling Psychologist*, 1975, 5, 10–14.

[11] Rogers and Stevens, *Person to Person*, p. 90.

[12] N. Raskin, *Studies on Psychotherapautic Orientation*. AAP Psychotherapy Research Monograph. Orlando, Florida: American Academy of Psychotherapy, 1974.

as a personal attack. Too many "misunderstandings" in life are just that—the failure to listen and try to understand another person's feelings and point of view. Empathy is probably the single most important attitude for improving our ability to listen and our working relationships with others.

EXERCISES

ACCEPTANCE.   In order to see how your attitudes affect your listening ability, select two people: one with whom you have good communication, and one with whom you normally do not. Then reflect on your attitude toward each of these people by asking yourself these questions:

- Do you feel this person has something worthwhile to say?
- Do you trust this person to express himself or herself honestly?
- Do you feel this person has the right to his or her own views?
- How warm and cordial are you with this person? Do you tend to be short and judgmental? Does your attitude fluctuate?

Since your attitude of acceptance as a listener creates a more favorable atmosphere for good communication, you should ask yourself if you are sufficiently accepting. You may want to monitor your attitudes toward the people with whom you have the most difficulty communicating.

SELF-ACCEPTANCE.   Look back over the dozen characteristics of people high in self-acceptance (pages 62–63), and ask yourself how much each one applies to you.

- In which characteristics are you the strongest?
- In which are you weakest?
- How do these strengths and weaknesses affect your listening ability?
- Do you tend to be defensive at times?
- Are you afraid of personal criticism?

Since the degree to which we accept ourselves affects our acceptance of others, the more aware of and comfortable we become with our limitations, the less they will interfere with our communication.

EMPATHETIC LISTENING. Think back to the last time you had a heated disagreement with someone, either at home or at the office. If you were accused of "not understanding" his or her views, so much the better—you will have more material to work on. Now try to assess the degree to which you listened empathetically by answering the following questions:

- What do you think the person's message was?
- Did you walk away without really understanding it?
- Were you talking "at" or "past" each other?
- Were you confused by each other's reactions?
- Did you get hung up on content, or on feelings?

Or:

- Did you use reflective listening skills?
- Did you:
  Clarify questions?
  Paraphrase views?
  Reflect feelings?
  Summarize the issues?
- Did you use the listening rule, restating each other's views before continuing with your own?

Remember that empathetic listening is most needed when you are emotionally involved, especially in disagreements and problem-solving.

COMMUNICATING EMPATHY. How well do you express empathy? Is it easy for you to do so? Or do you tend to do it only in intimate relationships? When was the last time you can recall expressing empathy? Was it in response to someone's grief? Or someone's joy or long-awaited success? Can you also express empathy in everyday communication?

Can you express empathy better with someone of your own or the opposite sex? Or does it depend more on the other person's personality or your degree of intimacy with them? Do you feel your ability to express empathy has been enhanced or limited by your sex role?

The next time it is appropriate to listen empathetically, whether in response to someone's deeply felt emotions or perhaps a mutual problem-solving situation, make an effort to communicate your empathy more effectively. Remember, this is done more through your actual use of reflective listening skills than simply by uttering sympathetic responses like "I understand," "Oh, dear," or "How awful!"

CHAPTER SIX

THE IMPORTANCE OF NONVERBAL COMMUNICATION

Our awareness of nonverbal communication is reflected in many of our popular figures of speech. We speak of happy people being "filled with joy" or "bursting with pride." We see fearful people as "paralyzed" or "frozen" with fear. Angry people may be described as "trembling with rage," "bursting at the seams," or "ready to explode." Tense people are portrayed as "biting their lips." In each of these examples, people are expressing their feelings through their bodies as well as their words. While experts differ in their estimates, it is safe to say that more than half of our face-to-face communication is nonverbal. Listening to the speaker's message, then, means learning how to read his or her body language as well.

READING BODY LANGUAGE

Essentially, nonverbal communication, popularly known as "body language," includes all those behavioral expressions that do not rely on words or word symbols.

Learning how to read these bodily expressions is important for several reasons. First, while words may readily convey factual knowledge, words alone are rarely adequate to express our feelings. Sometimes we say "I am not sure how to express this in words," meaning our feelings are more intense or somewhat more complex than we can find words for. Yet these unverbalized feelings are inevitably expressed in body language. Second, our body language also shows how we are coping with those feelings. If a speaker is having difficulty controlling her anger, she might raise her voice, turn away, or become physically aggressive. Third, body language tells us how people feel about us. A speaker who points, glares, or makes constant interruptions is conveying an entirely different feeling toward us than one who smiles and is relaxed and listens to us. Finally, nonverbal communication is especially valuable in that it tends to be unintentional or unconscious. That is, even though people measure their words, and sometimes control their facial expressions, there is often a "leakage" of masked feelings, perhaps in a facial expression, gesture, or tone of voice. Any of these nonverbal expressions may help us to confirm what is said verbally, or sometimes question it.

Two words of caution are in order. First, popular knowledge has it that nonverbal expressions have universal meaning, for example, folded arms always mean defensiveness. But this simply isn't true. Instead, specific nonverbal expressions like folded arms are best understood in relation to the particular situation in which they occur. For example, I once saw a hypnotist performer ask for volunteers to come onto the stage for a demonstration hypnosis. But among all those who raised their hands to volunteer, I noticed he selected only those who were sitting in a relaxed posture, with arms open, some even slouched down in their seats. He did not take anyone with crossed arms or legs. In both cases, he had read their body language to indicate their attitude toward hypnosis. I doubt that the hypnotist would have made the mistake of thinking all people with folded arms or crossed legs were generally overinhibited, neurotic people. Rather, he probably realized the first rule of understanding nonverbal communication—namely, that body language must be read in the context of the situation.

The other caution concerns not situation but cultural differences. Author Julius Fast tells of a fifteen-year-old Puerto Rican girl who had been caught in the washroom with a group of girls suspected of smoking. Although most of the others were known troublemakers, Livia had no record of trouble. Yet, after being interviewed by the principal she was found guilty. The principal referred to her suspicious attitude, expressed in not looking him in the eye. He took this as a sign of guilt. The incident led to protests of the mother and a demonstration of Puerto Rican parents at school the next morning. Fortunately, a Spanish teacher at the school, who knew Livia, told the principal that in Puerto Rico nice girls do not look directly at adults, as a sign of respect and obedience. The principal had misread Livia's nonverbal behavior. Perhaps the incident added an important item to his body language "vocabulary" so that he would no longer confuse shyness with guilt.[1]

Ordinarily, we achieve a more accurate understanding of a person's body language when we view it in relation to the particular situation as well as the person's social and cultural background. At the same time, some people are better than others in reading body language. Several studies have shown that women are more accurate both in sending and receiving nonverbal messages of emotion. Yet in one study, men who worked with people like psychiatrists, psychologists, and teachers as well as actors, artists, and designers scored as high as women.[2] That is, decoding body language is largely a learned ability. Then too, individuals of both sexes vary widely among themselves, with some people being good senders but poor receivers, and others just the opposite. Generally, our sensitivity to nonverbal messages increases with age and experience. How about yourself? Would you say you are getting better at reading body language? I hope the following pages will help you to gain a greater awareness of the meaning and importance of nonverbal expressions.

FACIAL EXPRESSIONS

Facial expressions are the major indicators of emotions. Positive emotions such as happiness, love, and surprise are the easiest to recognize. Negative emotions such as sadness, anger, and disgust

[1] Julius Fast, *Body Language* (New York: M. Evans and Company, Inc., 1970), p. 146ff.

[2] R. Rosenthal, et al, "Body Talk and Tone of Voice: The Language Without Words," *Psychology Today*, September 1974, pp. 64–68.

are usually the most difficult to recognize. The following facial expressions are often associated with these six basic emotions:

- Surprise: raised eyebrows, wide-opened eyes, dropped-opened mouth, parted lips.
- Fear: eyebrows raised and drawn together, eyes opened, corners of mouth drawn back, lips stretched, mouth may or may not be open.
- Anger: eyebrows pulled down, sometimes curved forehead wrinkles, eyes squinting, lips pressed together or bared teeth.
- Disgust: lowered eyebrows, wrinkled nose, mouth open with forward lower lip or mouth closed with upper lip pushed up by lower lip.
- Sadness: eyebrows drawn together, glazed eyes often with drooping upper lip, mouth either open or closed with outer corners pulled slightly down.
- Happiness: no distinctive eyebrows, relaxed eyes, outer corners of lips raised, usually drawn back.[3]

Portrait painters and photographers have long known that the human face is asymmetrical, with the result that the left and right sides of our face may express our emotions differently. Recent research explains that this is because each side of the face is under the control of a different side of the brain. While the left side of the brain controls speech and rational thought, the right side permits emotional, imaginative, and sensory activity. Each side crosses over, so that our normally dominant left side of the brain is expressed on the right side of our face giving that side a more controlled expression. Because the right side of our brain is expressed on the left side of our face, it is harder to disguise our feeling on the left side of the face. While positive emotions are expressed more evenly across both sides of the face, negative emotions are expressed more heavily on the left side. Since our left eye (from the "emotional" right side of the brain) is the best judge of emotions, when in doubt about a speaker's true feelings, you might try looking at the left side of the speaker's face with your left eye. In actual practice, however, both sides of our brain function to-

[3] P. Ekman, W. V. Friesen, and P. Ellsworth, *Emotion in the Human Face* (New York: Pergamon Press, 1972). Used by permission.

gether, so that these differences usually appear less pronounced than in subjects whose right and left hemispheres have been surgically separated.

The mouth and lips are especially expressive of people's feelings. We are all familiar with the pursed lips associated with deep thought, or the smirking lips that often accompany doubt or sarcasm. Smiling is mostly a social expression communicating a sense of pleasure, humor, friendliness, or the need for approval. For some reason, women generally smile more than men. At the same time, smiling behavior is also affected by regional and cultural differences, with southerners tending to smile more, while upstate New Yorkers and New Englanders smile less than average. Since smiling reflects more than one motive, we should be careful not to over-interpret a speaker's smiles. However, excessive smiling often expresses a need for approval or deference to authority. Smiling accompanied by raised eyebrows tends to express submissiveness, while infrequent smiling with lowered eyebrows tends to express dominance.

Because the face is so expressive of feelings, speakers often attempt to control or "mask" their facial expressions. For instance, when someone accidentally bumps into us or has made a mistake, he or she may feel as annoyed as we do, but smile instinctively as if to express a polite apology. In this case, the smile may be a bit "canned," or forced, betraying a mixture of annoyance and apology.

GAZING AND EYE CONTACT

Since most of what we learn comes through our visual sense, we are twice as likely to look while listening than while speaking. Looking is an extremely important part of communication. It not only shows the speaker we are interested; it also helps us to pay better attention to what is being said.

Interestingly, during a conversation both the speaker and the listener tend to adopt an alternate "look" and "look-away" pattern. It is as if constant looking would be too distracting to the speaker or to the listener's concentration. Both speaker and listener look at each other for anywhere from one to ten seconds. This is likely to occur immediately before or after the speaker says something. From time to time, the speaker's and listener's eyes will meet in eye contract, though these instances are usually of shorter duration than one-way gazing of either partner.

We are more apt to maintain eye contact with the speaker while discussing pleasant topics, like the recent accomplishment or our plans for the forthcoming weekend. On the other hand, we are more likely to avoid eye contact while discussing unpleasant or embarrassing topics, such as a mistake of either partner or the termination of the relationship. In the latter instance, avoidance of direct eye contact is an expression of politeness and consideration of the other's feelings. Excessive or inappropriate eye contact in times like these tend to be resented as an intrusion on one's privacy. Moreover, too much eye contact or staring is usually taken as a sign of hostility. The hostile significance of staring may be seen in the fact that animals usually stare at each other just before attacking.

We also need to be aware that looking reflects other aspects of the overall relationship. For instance, we tend to look more at those whom we admire or with whom we have a more intimate relationship. Also, women tend to have greater eye contact than men, probably because they feel more comfortable with intimacy. On the other hand, people avoid eye contact in competitive situations, lest this be construed as a sign of hostility. Furthermore, we tend to look more when we are at a distance from the speaker. The closer we get to the speaker, the more we avoid eye contact. Generally, eye contact helps speakers to feel they are communicating with us and to have a more favorable impression of us. But excessive or inappropriate gazing, including constant eye contact, often gives others a negative impression of us.

Looking helps to regulate conversation in a couple of ways. First of all, initial eye contact helps us to catch the speaker's eye. We often speak of the need to "catch the waiter's eye." As long as the speaker is using the alternate looking and looking away pattern, he or she probably hasn't finished speaking. When finished, a speaker tends to look directly at the listener as if to say "I am through, now it is your turn."

VOCAL EXPRESSIONS

A good listener "reads between the lines," hears more than the speaker's words. He also hears the speaker's pitch, tone of voice, and rate of speech. He notices the variations of speech, like failing to complete a sentence and/or pausing frequently. Next to the speaker's words and facial expressions, these vocal expressions are the most helpful clues to the speaker's message.

Tone of voice is an especially valuable clue to feelings. Rollo May, a famous psychotherapist, often asks himself "What does the voice say when I stop listening to the words and listen only to the tone?"[4] Feelings will be expressed regardless of the words that are spoken. People can accurately express their emotions even while reciting the alphabet! From the listener's standpoint, anger and sadness are usually the easiest to recognize, while nervousness and jealousy are among the most difficult.

The volume and pitch of the speaker's voice, how high or low or how loud or soft it sounds, are also helpful in decoding the speaker's message. Some emotions like enthusiasm, joy, and disbelief are usually delivered in a high pitch. Anger and fear are also expressed in a high pitch, as well as in a wider range of tone, pitch, and volume. On the other hand, emotions like sadness, grief, and apathy are usually expressed softly and in a low pitch, especially toward the end of each sentence.

The rate of speech also tells us something about the speaker's feelings. People talk faster when they are excited or anxious, or when they are speaking about a personal problem or something that is threatening to them. People are also apt to speak faster when they are trying to persuade us or sell us something. On the other hand, people usually talk more slowly when they are depressed, grief-stricken, disgusted, contemptuous, or when they are tired.

People unwittingly express their feelings and personalities through minor speech disturbances, such as repeating words, vacillating in their choice of words, or failing to complete a sentence. People tend to vacillate in choosing words when they are unsure

[4] Rollo May, *Love and Will* (New York: Dell Publishing Company, Inc., 1974), p. 239.

of themselves or are getting ready to surprise us. Those who stutter often speak perfectly well until they become anxious, then lapse into stuttering. Generally, these speech disturbances are more intrusive when the speaker feels anxious or is trying to deceive us.

The listener should also be aware of meanings expressed in vocal variations such as a groan, grunt, sigh, nervous cough, tongue-clicking, raspberry, and so on. The variety is endless. Again, it is essential to realize that more meaning can usually be expressed in sounds rather than words. This is also true of the language of gestures.

POSTURES AND GESTURES

People reveal their attitudes and feelings by the way they stand or sit, and the way they move various parts of their bodies.

We take it as a compliment when speakers lean toward us in a conversation, probably because this posture suggests they are attentive. On the other hand, we feel less favorable toward those who lean away from us or slouch down in their chairs while speaking with us. Generally, we feel more comfortable talking with someone who adopts a relaxed posture, although persons with a higher status than ours are more likely to adopt such a posture, probably they feel more secure in the relationship. That is, they will sit rather than stand, or they will recline or lean sideways rather than sit erect.

The angle at which people feel comfortable sitting or standing in relation to each other varies with the nature of the situation, or with sex and culture differences. When people know each other well or are in a cooperative situation, they generally prefer to stand or sit at a right angle to one another. When they are meeting strangers or are in a bargaining situation, they feel more comfortable in a face-to-face position. Women often prefer to converse with their partners at a slight angle or side-by-side, especially if they know them well. Men often prefer the face-to-face position, unless they are in a competitive situation. People in the United States and England generally prefer to position themselves at a right angle to their partners, while Swedes tend to avoid this position. On the other hand, Arabs prefer the head-on position.[5] If you are unsure which position your partners feel most comfortable in, watch where they stand, sit, or move their chairs when given the freedom to do so.

Many gestures of the arms or legs are somewhat obvious in meaning. For instance, crossed arms or legs usually signal a somewhat skeptical, defensive attitude, whereas uncrossed limbs express a more open, trusting attitude. Cupping one's hands under the chin is the sign of a thoughtful attitude. Putting hands on the hips may signal defiance or readiness to begin a task. Folding the arms behind one's head is an expression of dominance toward others.

People are constantly moving their heads throughout a conversation. While nodding the head does not always mean agreement, it does help the flow of conversation, as if giving the speaker permission to continue. Head nods also tend to reinforce the speaker, so that in a group speakers tend to speak more directly to those who consistently nod their heads. On the other hand, rapid nods or turning the head aside and gesturing with the hands often indicate to the speaker that a listener wishes to talk.

Generally, speakers and listeners alike prefer partners with animated facial expressions and expressive body movements. The frequent use of gestures on either person's part is taken as a sign of interest and friendliness, conveying positive feelings. An excessive use of gestures, however, may be an expression of anxiety or the lack of confidence in being able to communicate verbally.

PERSONAL SPACE

How close or far apart people space themselves in relation to each other is another important factor in communication. Sometimes we even speak of our relationships with others in spatial terms like "keeping our distance" from someone we dislike or fear, or "getting close" to someone we like. Generally, the more interested two people are in each other, the close together they sit or stand.

[5] John Lamberth, *Social Psychology* (New York: Macmillan Publishing Company, Inc., 1980).

But there is a definite limit to how close people will let others come. Studies have shown that the distance between people in conversation, at least in the United States, depends largely on the type of interaction, as follows:

- Intimate distance—(within 18″) This is appropriate for intimate behavior like lovemaking or wrestling, and is reserved for close friends or those in body contact sports.
- Personal distance—(1½ to 4′) for conversation between friends, with or without touching.
- Social distance—(4 to 12′) For informal social and business transactions, with more formal business transactions at the upper range.
- Public distance—(12′ and beyond) At this distance one may or may not acknowledge the other with a minimum of speaking without being rude.[6]

Generally, people feel more comfortable and form a more favorable impression of someone when they stand or sit within the appropriate distance for a given type of transaction. Getting too close or remaining too distant affects communication negatively. Also, the closer people get, the less they look at each other, as if to respect each other's privacy. And the further away they get, the more they look and use gestures while talking, as if to insure keeping the other's attention.

These rules vary considerably depending on other factors such as age, sex, and culture. For instance, children and old people prefer to come closer, while adolescents and middle-age people prefer more distance. Generally, women prefer standing or sitting closer to someone of either sex than men do, probably because women are more comfortable with intimate relationships. Personality is another factor, with people with high self-esteem coming closer, while more anxious, neurotic people keep further away. Status and power also affect the distance between people. We generally prefer greater distance between ourselves and those with higher status and power than us, while people of equal status come closer together. Culture is another factor. People from Latin American and Mediterranean countries tend to come closer to their part-

[6] E. A. Hall, "A System for the Notation of Proxemic Behavior," *American Anthropologist* (1963) 65:1003–26.

ners in conversation, while people from Northern European countries like the Swedes, Scots, and English keep more distant. Americans fall somewhere in between.[7]

Desks may also structure the distance between people when they are talking. A desk is generally associated with a position of authority, so that when a listener sits behind a desk it is likely to be more of a role transaction. While this may afford a sense of relief to some partners, it tends to inhibit others. For this reason, some administrators and executives prefer holding interviews and personal conferences in a conversation corner away from their desks, with two chairs positioned at an angle to each other.

RESPONDING TO NONVERBAL COMMUNICATION

Interestingly, one way we respond to a speaker's nonverbal communication is by unconsciously copying his or her posture and facial expressions. That is, when a speaker folds her arms or crosses her legs, we may find ourselves automatically adopting the same gestures. It may be that we are responding to the speaker with bodily empathy, as if to say "I am with you. Go ahead."

Verbally responding to a speaker's nonverbal communication is another matter. Ordinarily, we should respond to the speaker's nonverbal expressions in relation to his or her overall communication. That is, when a speaker's facial expressions, tone of voice, and posture are consistent with his or her words, there is no problem. Here, the bodily expressions help to drive home the spoken word, so that we are more certain to "get the message." When the nonverbal expressions conflict with the speaker's words, however, we tend to favor the former. As the popular saying goes, "Actions speak louder than words."

When there are minor discrepancies between a speaker's words and body language, as when someone hesitates several times in inviting us to something, we may or may not choose to respond verbally to these conflicting nonverbal expressions. A lot depends

[7] John Lamberth, *op. cit.*

on the people involved, the nature of their relationship, and the particular situation. But we rarely ignore these nonverbal expressions. Instead, conflicting body signals often lead us to delay action on a request or to have second thoughts after the conversation is ended. In other words, the nonverbal tends to register with us, often with a lag in time. Consequently, when we are getting "mixed signals" from a speaker, we may choose to say something like. "I will think it over" or "I will get back to you on this," giving us time to evaluate the speaker's overall communication before making a firm decision.

When there are marked discrepancies between a speaker's words and nonverbal signals, a verbal response to the mixed message may be in order. Perhaps the most skillful example of this comes from Dr. Fritz Perls' practice of Gestalt therapy, in which he deliberately observes and responds to the patient's nonverbal expressions as an integral part of bringing about therapeutic self-understanding. For example, in one training film, Dr. Perls called attention to a woman patient's fidgeting with her hands, squirming in her seat, and nervously smiling and giggling. He pointed out that such behavior masked her feelings of dependency and her attempts to manipulate him to give her the answers. Even though the patient initially responded in a defensive manner, she eventually became more aware of her feelings and manipulative behavior with authority figures.

Ordinarily, it is advisable to respond to a speaker's conflicting nonverbal expressions with much greater tact. For example, if a speaker has agreed to do something for you but is giving off mixed signals of doubt, such as frequent pauses, questions, or puzzled facial expressions, you may choose to respond to the latter by saying something like "You seem a bit skeptical about this. Would you like to talk about it?" Such a tactful response shows that you are attentive to the speaker's overall communication but in a way that does not arouse that person's anxiety and defensiveness. It simply provides the speaker with an opportunity to express himself or herself more fully.

To summarize, the art of listening effectively depends on more than an accurate comprehension of the speaker's words. Communication also includes nonverbal signals which may confirm, or sometimes negate, the spoken message. Being sensitive to these nonverbal meanings will help listeners make the right interpretations and responses for more efficient and satisfying overall communication.

EXERCISES

OBSERVING FACIAL EXPRESSIONS.   The idea for this exercise comes from an experience I had as I was writing this chapter. I was about to take our younger daughter on an errand, and had already gotten into the car and started the motor. As our daughter left the front door, however, she turned to speak with my wife and continued talking and talking. After getting over my momentary irritation, I began observing their gestures and facial expressions. I tried to guess what they were talking about. When our daughter finally came to the car, I asked "Were you two disagreeing about something?" "Yes," she said, "but how did *you* know?" "Aha," I replied, "by watching your face and gestures."

Try doing the same thing yourself as an exercise in observing facial expressions. Next time you have the opportunity, select two people you know in a conversation that you can observe but not hear. Carefully observe their body language, paying special attention to facial expressions. Can you determine what they are talking about? Which facial expressions were the best clues? Were smiles and frowns especially helpful? What feelings were being expressed? If possible, ask one or both of the people involved to see how accurate your estimate was. Does this exercise demonstrate how much of our communication depends on nonverbal expressions?

LOOKING AND LISTENING.   The purpose of this exercise is to make you more aware of the relationship between looking and listening. This exercise can be done either by observing others or yourself while in conversation.

If you observe other people, answer the following questions:

- Did both people "look" and "look away" throughout the conversation?
- How much direct eye contact did they have?

- Did each person look more while listening than while talking?
- When finished speaking, did the speaker look at the listener, signaling "It's your turn"?

If you are observing your own conversation, answer the same questions about yourself and your partner. Did each of you tend to look more while listening than while talking? Did you find that looking helps you to pay better attention while listening?

LISTENING TO THE TONE OF VOICE. This exercise is based on Rollo May's suggestion that we need to listen to the speaker's tone of voice apart from his or her words. It is especially suited for a telephone conversation, where there fewer distractions than in face-to-face communication.

Next time someone is trying to express their feelings to you, whether on the telephone or not, pay special attention to their tone of voice. How would you characterize the speaker's voice? Does his or her pitch and tone of voice match the verbal message? Or does the voice say something different than the words? Does the tone of voice seem appropriate for the type of transaction? Do you also find that some individuals characteristically speak in one tone of voice, like a monotone or an agitated or excited voice?

A variation of this exercise is to express some of your own feelings into a tape recorder. Then play it back and concentrate on listening to your tone of voice. How would you characterize it? Does it command attention? Does it sound dull? Would you agree that the tone of voice expresses our feelings too?

BECOMING AWARE OF POSTURES AND GESTURES. This exercise can be done either by observing others or yourself in conversation. Either way, the main point is to become more aware of how we position ourselves and use gestures as a way of expressing ourselves in relation to others. If you are observing others, answer the following questions:

- What are the partners expressing in their posture?
- Is their bodily attitude "open" or "closed"?
- What are they doing with their arms? their hands?

- How are they arranging their legs?
- Notice how they move their heads. Do the head movements help the flow of conversation?

A fun way to do this exercises is to watch a film without sound, trying to guess what is being expressed in body language alone. Then play the film again with the words added. How well did you do? Deaf people tend to do especially well on this exercise, mostly because of their heightened reliance on the visual sense.

HOW CLOSE DO PEOPLE GET TO YOU?   To find out, select a convenient day, and then each time someone initiates a conversation with you, make a mental note of how close to you they stand or sit. If you are sitting at a desk, you may measure the distance between your desk and the other person's chair. Then watch to see if someone pulls the chair closer or further away. Observe how the spatial distance between others and yourself depends on the following influences:

- Type of transaction
- Liking for each other
- Status or authority
- Sex, age
- Social, cultural background

In many cases, spatial distance will not make a marked difference in the communication. Were there any instances when the distance did make a noticeable difference? Was it when someone came too close? Did this make you feel uncomfortable? Or did it depend a lot on the particular person?

CHAPTER SEVEN

REMEMBERING WHAT YOU HEAR

Perhaps you have had the experience of asking a friend or a colleague a simple question like "What time are we meeting this morning?" only to have the reply "I just told you, weren't you *listening?*" Experiences like this make us feel foolish. Yet each of us has done this sort of thing at one time or another. Sometimes, we weren't really listening in the first place. At other times we listened well enough, but quickly forgot what we heard. In the latter case, the problem is *remembering* what we hear.

In this chapter we will explain how memory works and offer some practical suggestions for improving your memory habits in order that you may listen more effectively.

HOW YOUR MEMORY WORKS

Human memory—the ability for storing and retrieving information—has been compared to a filing system, a magic slate, a telephone switchboard, and most recently, a computer. Yet our capacity for memory is far greater than the most impressive computers ever built. And scientists have yet to figure out how human memory can retrieve so much information as quickly and as often as it does. Despite the continued technological improvements in computers, our human memory remains capable of even greater understanding and creativity in solving problems. You might say "Well, computers

87

don't have emotions to interfere with memory." But emotions may also serve a positive role in memory as we shall see a little further on.

We often speak of memory as if it were a thing. Yet it is more of a process—information processing, to be exact—than something localized in our head. To be sure, the brain and nervous system are basic components of our memory. But memory is also integrally involved with our knowledge, past experience, and emotions.

Attention, the condition of readiness through selective focusing of consciousness, is the mechanism that regulates the input of data into our memory. Out of the overwhelming amount of sensory and verbal signals that bombard our senses, our attention admits only a fraction of it for further processing. So much of what we hear goes right by us. Only what we listen to, or consciously pay attention to, is processed in our memory.

THE THREE LEVELS OF MEMORY

The processing of data in the human memory bank takes place on three overlapping levels. These are commonly referred to as sensory storage, short-term memory, and long-term memory.

The sensory storage is the brief delay between sensory impressions and their dissipation, usually about one- to five-tenths of a second. For example, clinch your first, then quickly open your hand and notice the faint trace of your fingers in your palm. As this disappears so does the sensation of pressure fade, and is gone. Or tap your fingers on a hard surface and notice how the sound becomes less distinct as it fades away. Fortunately, the constant bombardment of our sensory system comes and goes, with little or no record in our memory. As you would expect, this protects our sensory system from becoming overburdened with useless data. When we have experienced something in a novel or intense way, such as the unexpected sound of a gunshot, we usually remember it longer. But this is more because of the feelings it arouses and the associations with other aspects of our memory. After living or working with someone for a long time, and after that person has gone or moved to another job, we may find ourselves saying something like "I can just hear old George telling me how he did this job. . . ." Again, because of associations in our memory, we tend to hold some sensory memories longer than others.

Short-term memory is another word for our attention span. It enables us to retain different types of information than strictly sensory, including visual images, verbal information, and concepts. While the sensory cells in our ears retain the sensation of sounds of what we hear, the short-term memory captures the meaning, or interpretation of these words in context. Yet our attention span is also very limited both in *time*—usually less than thirty seconds—and in its capacity for the *number* of items retained—thought to be about seven items, plus or minus two. So if someone gives you the names of ten people over the phone, chances are you will remember only about five or six at the most, and frequently fewer. Fortunately, you can improve your short-term memory through time-tested strategies, which we will discuss shortly.

Long-term memory refers to the storage and retrieval of information for long-term use. This is what most people mean when they refer to their "memory." In order to store things in your long-term memory, you not only have to listen, but deliberately process the information in greater depth. This usually means rehearsing the information, associating it with something else you know, or using the information in some way. Unlike short-term memory, which is an in-and-out system, long-term memory involves neurological and chemical changes, which account for its greater permanence. Just how permanent and accurate our long-term memory is is a matter of debate. Psychologists like Sigmund Freud and Carl Jung held that many long-term memories lay deep in the unconscious, relatively undisturbed by conscious thoughts. Also, Wilder Penfield, a neurosurgeon, while examining an epileptic woman, accidentally found that electrical stimulation of the brain set off a vivid, re-experience of past events, suggesting that humans retain permanent imprints on the brain. Yet Elizabeth Loftus claims that most unassisted attempts at recollection evoke the same mixture of fiction and fact characteristic of memory as a whole.[1]

[1] Loftus, E. F. *Memory.* Reading, Mass.: Addison-Wesley Publishing Company, 1980.

FORGETTING

Even when we have listened to something and remembered it, we often forget it in due time. A typical forgetting curve shows that we forget most of what we hear almost as soon as we hear it, but also that we remember some of it a long time. A lot depends on how novel and interesting the information is, how useful it appears to us, how it affects us emotionally, and so forth.

The biggest single reason we forget something is interference. That is, some information interferes with other information. A simple illustration is when you are confronted with a great deal of similar information at once. For example, suppose you are introduced to five or six people in quick succession, say at a conference or party. By the time you have gotten to the last person, you have probably forgotten most of the names of the others. This is known as the serial effect, in which we tend to recall the last or most recent items best and the first items next best. We are more likely to forget items in the middle because our memory of them is interfered with from both sides, so to speak, by the earlier and later items. Later, we will suggest some ways of using this principle to your advantage. At this point, we suggest that if you want something remembered by someone else, tell them first; or if you want them to do something right away, save it for last.

Another major reason we forget has to do with our emotions, especially anxiety. This is because anxiety interferes most of all. In the first place, anxiety interferes with listening and storage of information. The simplest example is when you are listening to criticism or personal accusations. Chances are, you become so flustered that you block out much of what is said, or at least distort it. The same thing happens when you are trying to recall anxiety-arousing material. That is, you experience "failures" or lapses of memory. When you have been approached by your superior, no matter what his or her attitude, you probably have had the experience of "drawing a blank" in trying to give information that is part of your job to have on the tip of your tongue. The usual explanation is anxiety. A highly annoyed or angered supervisor only compounds the anxiety. In these instances, it is best to reassure others that the information will come back to you as soon as you quit trying so hard. Then, as you turn to another task, the desired information often pops into your head effortlessly, mostly because the anxiety is gone.

THE ALL-IMPORTANCE OF ATTENTION

The key to remembering what you hear is learning to pay better attention. But first, you must understand how attention works.

Every minute of our waking life we are taking in various sensory data. Sights, sounds, smells, touch, taste—all enter our various sensory channels simultaneously. Once we focus our attention on any one of these sensory data, though, the others recede from awareness. When you are momentarily preoccupied with reading something, you become a little less aware of the sounds around you. But once the telephone rings and you begin talking with someone on the phone, your attention shifts in favor of your ears, and you become less observant of what you see. This selective shifting of attention from one sensory channel to another is known as "sensory gating." An especially dramatic example of sensory gating is what happens when one sensory channel becomes overloaded and completely blocks out competing sensations.

SELECTIVE ATTENTION

When this shifting of attention occurs within a particular sensory channel, it is known as "selective attention." Perhaps you have had the experience of attending a meeting or a crowded party in which several people are trying to talk at once. It is impossible to hear any one of them clearly. What usually happens is that you pay attention to one person at a time, perhaps because of your interest in that person, familiarity, or that person's status. Only then, with some effort, do you manage to screen out all the sounds but those you are interested in. The capacity for selective attention is, of course, closely related to the human faculty of concentration, which blocks out not only sensory data but also interference from intruding mental processes.

What about the sounds you are not listening to? Do you miss them? Probably not. In experiments with "shadowing," people wearing earphones are asked to repeat aloud (shadow) each word as they hear it. Then at the same time they are exposed to another message in the other ear. As you might expect, subjects tend to recall a high percentage of the material they are listening to. Yet, it has also been shown that they record something of the other messages too, but more at the level of hearing than of listening. That is, people can usually tell whether a human voice was present, whether it was the voice of a man or a woman, and report other signals like a siren or bell, but they do not recall the content of the message. Yet, if such subjects are asked to recall the nonshadowed words immediately after they are heard, they can recall the last few items, showing that we do hear things we are not listening to, but only to a limited extent. Such material is dissipated after only a few seconds.[2]

An interesting example of shadowing is the highly skilled work done by simultaneous interpreters at the United Nations. They must listen, mentally translate, and speak, all at the same time. This is similar to what happens when you are trying to listen to someone and think or write at the same time. For instance, try to take notes while listening to a speaker. You may find yourself torn between thinking about what has just been said and trying to understand what is being said at present. It is very frustrating as we have all discovered. The reason is that the current data tends to enter our system automatically, yet trying to retain and record something said a few moments back demands a more complex processing of concepts, which in turn tends to compete with our attention to what we are hearing.

Consequently, it is often better to record accurately what we hear, making certain we understand it, before attempting to remember it. When you are dealing with simple information, like recording a telephone number, you can do both things at once. but when you are dealing with more complicated matters, like an intricate

---

[2] Peter H. Lindsay and Donald A Norman, *Human Information Processing* (2nd. edition). New York: Academic Press, 1977.

problem situation, it is better not to try writing too much while listening. Some note-taking aids memory and understanding. But excessive note-taking in such circumstances is self-defeating. Obviously, note-taking is easier when the speaker goes more slowly.

UNDERSTANDING WHAT YOU HEAR

Once you have begun paying attention to a verbal message, it is vital that you understand what you hear. For understanding is the key to both listening and memory.

As you read this page, chances are that your eyes are moving from one spot on the page to another several times a second, taking in whole words and phrases. This is because we read in terms of larger, more meaningful units than just letter by letter. In much the same way, we listen to meaningful phrases and sentences, not just a series of sounds. This is why we sometimes mistakenly hear something that wasn't said, because the entire phrase sounded like something we have heard before.

Another way of saying this is that we listen with our minds as well as our ears. We are able to listen, and to remember, because of the great wealth of knowledge and past experience we bring to each new situation. In a sense, we hear what we are prepared to hear, in many instances even what we expect to hear. In other words, it is the overall context that often determines the meaning of what we hear and remember. This is why it is so hard to listen in a new context—to strangers, to new dialects, new subjects, or people in another culture. We also, I might add, listen more carefully in these instances.

It is also true that the better we understand something, the easier it is to remember it. This has been brought out in numerous studies in which people remember different types of material to different degrees. People usually have difficulty remembering numbers, especially long ones like their automobile serial numbers, because numbers themselves are essentially meaningless. We do much better remembering narrative or prose passages, like a story or newspaper account of something. The easiest material to recall, of course, are the short, pithy slogans and jingles used in advertising, which is the main reason for their use. But the prime example is the memory of your own personal experience. It is usually easy to recall something you have done, especially when it has been highly rewarding for you, because personal experience is highly meaningful to each of us.

It is important that you understand what you hear at the moment you hear it. Otherwise, it may become lost through short-term memory. This is why it is wise to clear up right away any misunderstanding you may have. Ask the speaker to explain what he or she means, if not right away, then as soon as possible. For the better you understand something, the more easily and effortlessly you will recall it. That is because the same associations that make for understanding also aid memory.

LISTENING WITH YOUR EYES AND EARS

Your memory makes use of visual as well as verbal mechanisms, though experts differ on just how these two memory tracks are related.

Traditionally, the emphasis has been on visual memory. There is an old adage that a picture is worth a thousand words. Proof of this can be seen in studies in which people have been shown thousands of pictures of human faces, and then asked to recognize those pictures when paired with others they have never seen. Accurate recognition has been demonstrated up to 90 percent, much more impressive than with a similar number of names.[3] At the same time, hearing memory, at least in humans, may be stronger than touch, sight, or smell memory. People undergoing surgery have been known to recall things said while they were under anesthesia, much to others' chagrin.

Both visual and verbal memory tracks have their respective strengths. It seems that retrieval from verbal memory occurs much faster, but visual memory is more lasting. Just think how many words you can say versus how many you can read in the same length of time. Each type of memory is better under different cir-

[3] L. Standing, "Learning 10,000 Pictures." *Quarterly Journal of Experimental Psychology*, 1973, 25, 207–222.

cumstances. Concrete information is better retained through the use of visual imagery, while abstract ideas and concepts are better retained when heard.

All this has implications for the way you use your memory. Concrete data, like telephone numbers, faces, and names are best remembered through use of visual aids. It pays to write down such things. Yet concepts, principles, and ideas are best remembered after being explained and understood in conversation. Most effective of all is a combination of visual and verbal images, with optimal note-taking.

LISTENING AND YOUR SHORT-TERM MEMORY

We have already indicated that your short-term memory is just another name for your attention span, and that it lasts only half a minute or so and holds only about seven items. This means that improving your short-term memory consists in paying better attention. Fortunately, there are some time-honored strategies for doing this.

REPEAT WHAT YOU HEAR

When you are introduced to two or three people at a time, do you usually forget all the names right away? Most of us do because of short-term memory, and its mutual interference of the names with each other. Try to take enough time to keep each name separately from the others (as the people themselves are distinct from each other and not just a group). If you do not remember a person's full name, simply ask that person to repeat it. The sooner you do this the less embarrassing it is. Then when you hear it repeated, say the name aloud, preferably several times during your conversation with this person. Don't be embarrassed, it is a fact that we all love the sound of our own name! Many people dealing with the public, particularly in sales, have mastered this. If you are not carrying on a conversation with this person, simply repeat the name to yourself. But it is crucial to do this in the first minute or so. Otherwise, you have already lost it from your short-term memory. You can always ask the person again, but it becomes increasingly embarrassing with each request.

The same strategy works with all kinds of other important information, like dates, places, and numbers. When someone gives you a telephone number over the phone, it is easy to write it down with a wrong digit. Simply repeating it back not only helps you recall it better but also may serve to correct the mistake. If a mistake has been made, be sure to repeat it again, correctly. Another way of repeating information is simply to write it down. The act of writing it down not only aids your short-term memory, but also gives you a written record for long-term retention.

CONDENSE THE INFORMATION

Since our attention span can capture only about seven items at a time, it helps to condense information into as few *meaningful* units as possible. For instance, suppose someone in conversation with you (1) asks for some information, (2) complains about a problem, and (3) requires some type of response. It helps to group the items into separate units corresponding to (1) information needed, (2) problems, and (3) action required.

FORM MEANINGFUL ASSOCIATIONS

This is a key strategy for better recall, sometimes referred to as mnemonic devices (from Greek, "to remember"). These are succinct ways of creating meaningful associations with material that is otherwise difficult to remember. For instance, each fall and spring most of us would forget which may turn our clocks, but we can remember correctly with the use of a simple verbal mnemonic device: "Spring ahead, fall back," which translates into turning your clock ahead one hour in the spring and back an hour in the fall.

Visual mnemonic devices are also helpful. For instance, a bank advertised that you could get an automobile loan by simply dialing

CAR-LOAN. I would have long forgotten the telephone number from the numbers alone, but the obvious association between the number and purpose of calling it remains vivid even today. Both visual and verbal mnemonic devices are extremely helpful in improving your memory.

CODE COMPLEX INFORMATION

This involves organizing the information around some recognizable symbols. The use of numbers is a good example. When recording someone's social security number, it is much easier to remember it as broken down into familiar, manageable units, such as 238–38–1041 than as a single number 238381041. In the latter case, the numbers run together, making them harder to remember. Telephone numbers are also more easily remembered through use of various codes, whether area codes or local exchanges. In Philadelphia, where I live, you can get weather information by dialing WE (first two letters of "weather") 6–1212. If you want the correct time, you simply dial the same number preceded by TI (the first two letters of "time"). Recognizing similarities helps us to remember not only numbers, but also names.

There are many ways to code information. Numbers are best grouped in their familiar forms or smaller units, such as telephone numbers and social security numbers. Names may be coded by a short association with the person's organization or task to be done.

USE IT OR LOSE IT

It is true with memory as with so many other things: the more you use something, rehearse it periodically, and apply it, the better you retain it.

In a meeting one evening, someone asked me for the telephone numbers of several other members of that organization. I wrote them down rapidly one after the other. One woman was astonished. "How do you remember all those numbers?" she asked. I replied simply that I had used all those numbers repeatedly over a period of several months, to the point the numbers were always handy. You have probably had a similar experience. Think of types of information you use habitually—names of people, company names, addresses, and so forth. If you use them regularly, you will recall them better.

At the same time, I have *heard* instructions about how to use something, say a mimeograph machine, which I have trouble remembering. When I use the device only occasionally, I find I must ask someone who uses it regularly "How do I use this?" Bystanders who are accustomed to using it will smile, thinking I am lacking in brains. But memory fades quickly with infrequent use, no matter how smart we are.

In both instances, the principle is the same: "Use it or lose it." The more you repeat, use, or apply what you hear, the better you will retain it.

STORING AND RETRIEVING INFORMATION

When you want to retain information for a long time you must transfer it to your long-term memory. As we explained earlier, this involves processing the information to greater depth. First, you must rehearse the information sufficiently so that it will not be lost from your short-term memory. You must also form meaningful and lasting associations with the material, associations with data you already have stored in your memory, however remote. All of this involves two related processes, the storing and retrieving of information.

STORING INFORMATION

The first thing to note about adding something to your long-term memory, is that it is not a passive slate or storage tank. Memory is an active, integrative process involving your attitudes and emotions as well as cognitive processes. Memory is not just in your head; it is also a function of your personality and motivation. In order to remember better, you must work at it. Consider the following suggestions.

DO YOU WANT TO REMEMBER SOMETHING? If you do, you are much more likely to do so. Perhaps you have had the experience of meeting someone you were quite interested in or impressed by. How effortlessly you recalled that person's name, address, or the like! Such "instant memory" simply shows how easily you can recall what you want to. On the other hand, you tend to "forget" unpleasant or embarrassing things. You also tend to remember things which seem useful to you. There is also a tendency to remember interrupted or incompleted tasks better than completed ones. It is as if some interior monitor, in conjunction with our total personality, decides what we shall remember. But attitude has a lot to do with it.

ORGANIZE YOUR INFORMATION. Next to motivation, this is the most important aspect of memory. The more effectively you categorize and store information, the more likely you can retrieve it when you want to. Like a computer, your memory can set up and use "cross-files," through visual imagery, mnemonic devices, coding, and so forth. Group similar items together and, whenever possible, put them into some kind of logical order.

UNDERSTAND WHAT YOU HEAR. As stated earlier, the more meaningful the information, the better you retain it, especially at the time you hear it. When something is not clear to you, ask the speaker about it *right away*. If this is not possible, do so as soon as you can. Also, ask yourself if the item makes sense to you or not. If the information does not make sense to you, chances are you won't remember it. Try to relate it to the overall sequence of what you hear. Does it logically follow what has been said? Does it fit?

DON'T TRY TO REMEMBER TOO MUCH AT ONCE. We learn better when we don't try to absorb too much at a time. A period of rest not only offsets boredom and fatigue but also interference with learning, for a resting period, however brief, allows us to absorb the earlier material before adding new learning. Perhaps this is why we take breaks between lectures or meetings, or space out our telephone calls. Just as cramming is a poor policy at school, so is it at the office. Also, it is true that sleeping on something overnight helps us to retain it better, for many of the same reasons mentioned above.

USE WHAT YOU HAVE LEARNED.   Here again is the value of rehearsal. The more you actively use information, the better you insure you will remember it when needed. Repeat the information back to the person who said it, say it to yourself, write it down, summarize it. All of these strategies will increase your retention.

RETRIEVING INFORMATION

There are three types of information retrieval: recognition, recall, and relearning. In recognition, you are presented with something and asked if you have seen or heard it before, as in a multiple choice test. In recall, you are given a cue and asked to come up with something which corresponds with it, as in an essay test. Since there are fewer cues in recall, it is more difficult than recognition. In relearning, you will find it easier to relearn material learned earlier than to learn new material, showing that you have retained more than you thought you had.

Since the storing and retrieving of information are intimately related, the better we store something, the more efficiently we can retrieve or "remember" it. You can improve your long-term memory by using many of the principles already mentioned for storing information. We will repeat several of the most important ones here.

Organize the information. This is the key to better memory. Sometimes the organization will be readily apparent in the material itself. At other times you will have to organize the material to suit your own purpose. For example, I have never had trouble remembering where to put things away in our kitchen since my wife told me the rationale of what goes in which drawer. One drawer contains utensils for "preparing" food, another for "serving" food. The organizing principle here is the function of the utensil. Such organization greatly aids memory.

Understand what you are trying to remember. This can hardly be overemphasized, since the most meaningful something is to you, the easier it is to remember. This means that in order to remember something better you must process the information to a greater depth than is needed for short-term memory. Consider the physical characteristics of the material, sound patterns, its meaning, how it all fits together, and so forth. The more deeply information is processed, the better you can recall it later.

Use contextual cues. Context provides a powerful cue for memory because of the presence of many associations or memory bonds. For example, suppose I ask you "What were you doing on your vacation five years ago?" At first you might say "That's ridiculous, nobody can remember that far back." But when you start mentally recreating the context of your life at that time, such as where you were, whom you were with, and so forth, you will be surprised at how much you can remember. This is the most common method, too, for trying to find a lost article. That is, we think back to the last time we had it, where we were, and what we were doing, then begin retracing our steps forward, using the context of our behavior as the cue. It works, doesn't it?

Work at improving your memory; it seldom comes easily for anyone. A good memory requires attention, effort, and skill. Furthermore, the more you know, the more capacity you have for memory, so that memory improves, rather than deteriorates with age and experience. Yet each of us has to fight the myth that memory efficiency fades with age. Such a notion survives mostly because of a "self-fulfilling prophecy": When a twenty-five-year old forgets a telephone number, one usually laughs it off, but when this happens to someone much older, he or she thinks "My memory is slipping." Such a person then makes less effort to remember and thus has a poorer recall. Don't believe the myth. Your memory is as good as you make it.

WHEN MEMORY FAILS

There are a variety of reasons why everyone's memory fails at one time or another.

Whenever you have something on "the tip of your tongue,"

for instance, but can't recall the correct word or name, you usually try to recapture it by saying several sounds that are similar. But unless you happen to hit on the correct name by pure chance, these false recalls don't actually help you. In these instances you can jog your memory through the use of visual, meaningful, or contextual cues.

When your memory of a past event disagrees with those of others who were present at that event, it could be because each of you saw the event differently in the first place. Conflicting accounts because of differences in perception are common among courtroom witnesses. But we often recall the same event differently because human memory serves our own needs, desires, and self-images. That is, memory is more a mixture of fact and fiction than we like to admit. We tend to rework all that is in our memory, so that each recall of the past gets more imaginative and less reliable.

I once worked with a group that included a man who had what we thought to be a most annoying habit. Whenever we referred back to something that had happened months earlier, each of us would attempt to recall the matter, correct each other's memory, and then act on the consensus of our recollections. But not this man. He always insisted on checking the written record. When he did, more often than not we discovered that the written record was more accurate, reminding us of the value of writing things down for better long-term memory.

Anxiety and emotions also play a powerful role in our memories. In the first place, emotions aid memory in the tendency to recall what we "want" to recall, including interrupted tasks. Yet this latter tendency holds true only for tasks performed under non-stressful conditions. When the unfinished business is something unpleasant or threatening to our self-esteem, anxiety blocks our memory. We have all discovered how difficult it is to recall painful, anxiety-arousing material.

The presence of anxiety also explains why we forget when we try too hard to remember. The harder you try, the more "blank" your mind becomes. At such times it is better to turn to something else momentarily, and before long, or perhaps the next day, the desired memory will return when it is not being forced.

Most failures of memory occur because we have never stored

the information properly in the first place. One executive, exasperated at the way matters were discussed at meetings but never acted
upon, improved listening effectiveness with the following simple
strategy. He designated a person to write down each point as it
was discussed. Then those items which needed to be acted upon
were summarized at the close of the meeting, together with the
names of the people responsible for doing them. After that, everyone began remembering more of what they heard.

EXERCISES

MEMORIZING A SERIES.   Try this exercise with a friend or colleague. Take a list of about a dozen names. Have your friend read
any two of them aloud, as if you were being introduced to these
people at a party. Then you are to repeat them back to your friend.
The next time your friend reads *three* new names from the list
and you repeat them back. Then any four names, and so on, increasing the number and mixing the order in which they are given.
How many names in a series did you remember? Were the last
and first names given recalled better than the others? Were the
names from the middle more difficult to remember? You can take
turns practicing this with each other, and you will be surprised
at your improvement.

USING MNEMONIC AIDS TO MEMORY.   Take some item you are
having difficulty remembering, such as a telephone number. Now
compose some sort of mnemonic device to help you remember
it. When possible, try to form some sort of meaningful association
between the position of the numbers and your mnemonic device.

For instance, the telephone number for Channel 10, a local
TV station, is 639–7836, which has a natural mnemonic, NEWS-
TEN. What does your own telephone number spell? Most of these
are barely pronounceable, but still they may be easier to recall
than the digits of the phone numbers. You can refer to the chart
below in constructing your mnemonic phone number devices. Test
them for a few weeks to see if they help you to recall the numbers
you use.

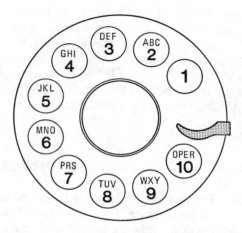

LISTENING WHILE YOU WRITE.   Turn on a news broadcast on your radio and start taking notes. The object is to get as much accurate information in three minutes as possible so that you could repeat it to someone else. Afterwards, answer these questions:

- Did you take time to understand what you heard before writing it down?
- Did you write only key words and phrases, or did you try to write sentences?
- While you were writing, did you try to keep on listening so that you wouldn't miss any essential facts?
- Is your reporting accurate and complete? (To check it you can listen to a repeat broadcast later.)

If what you have written is not accurate or complete enough to make sense when you repeat it, try this exercise again. Practice it until you understand how the act of writing interferes with listening, and how you can deal with this problem.

Secretaries who take shorthand, of course, are accustomed to writing as they listen. If you are in this category, here is another version of the exercise: Try writing the alphabet *backwards* while you listen to the news, then repeat as much of the news as you can remember!

MOTIVATION AND LONG-TERM MEMORY. This exercise deals with two types of material that are stored in your memory. The first (A) includes things people have said to you that you remember vividly. The second (B) includes things people have said to you that you have trouble recalling.

You will have no trouble recalling several instances of the type A material. Perhaps you remember the exact words that were used in some cases. What do all these "messages" have in common, aside from the fact that you remember them? Do you enjoy remembering them? Were they pleasant occasions? Did they add something special to your understanding at the time, for which you were grateful? Of course, good news travels fast; it also remains more secure in our memory, because we enjoy recalling it from time to time.

The type B material is recalled with much more difficulty. Can you think of something you would really prefer to forget? It is hard, because you have no desire to relive an unpleasant experience. What someone may have said to you years ago may have offended you at the time, or created anxiety that interfered with your performance. If it was someone telling you bad news, chances are you did not want to dwell on it.

Sometimes we forget things we really ought to remember, and remember things we could just as well do without. How does *your* memory do its selecting? What is its motivation?

CHAPTER EIGHT

YOU CAN BECOME A BETTER LISTENER

Throughout this book, we have stressed that listening, as opposed to hearing, is a learned skill. At the same time, we pointed out that listening is the least taught and least mastered of all the communications skills. Yet it is the skill most frequently called upon. Small wonder that most people rate themselves as only average listeners or worse.

We have emphasized that you can change your listening habits. In the preceding chapters we have explained how you can improve your listening by using the techniques of nonreflective and reflective listening and adopting a more accepting and empathetic attitude toward the speaker. We have also stressed attentiveness to the nonverbal aspects of communication as well as better memory habits.

At this point, we would like to put all these things in perspective. We will point out the importance of selecting the appropriate kind of listening, which changes from one situation to the next. Partly by way of summary, we will also list the Dos and Don'ts of listening, along with some of the risks and rewards of listening.

APPROPRIATE LISTENING

People communicate for all sorts of reasons, some of which are not always clear to themselves, much less to others. Sometimes they are simply being sociable, and we should not take them literally. At other times, they want to communicate information, which means we have to listen more carefully to their words. Then, again, people sometimes use words to express their feelings and attitudes, which demand more active listening skills. In still other instances they are busily persuading us to do something. In each case, it is important that we gear our listening to the purpose of the speaker's communication. Otherwise we misunderstand each other.

In the following pages, we will delineate four purposes of communication: social, informational, expressive, and persuasive.[1] As you read, keep in mind that speakers often shift from one purpose to another without warning, or may be communicating for more than one purpose.

1. *Social communication.* When the purpose of communication is primarily social, people speak to acknowledge each other's presence and to maintain their relationships with each other rather than to convey content. This usually involves a certain amount of ritual communication, such as saying the "expected" things, engaging in "small talk," and exchanging the common courtesies of life. People tend to present themselves in a favorable light and avoid revealing things they do not want others to know about them. Furthermore, they take it for granted that others will do the same. In this sense, much social communication consists of the management of surface impressions, often at the cost of honest self-disclosure.

Listening appropriately at this level begins with our willingness to take part in the rituals of everyday communication. The failure to do so may jeopardize our relationships with others. Sometimes all that is needed is a nonverbal response, such as a smile or a raised hand. At other times, we are expected to speak. Social communication involves taking turns talking and listening, or at least not interrupting. It also means we do not take everything we hear at face value. When someone asks, "Hi, how are you?" we do not give a literal, detailed account of our problems. We

[1] *Your Personal Listening Profile.* Sperry Corporation, 1980.

simply indicate our feelings as succinctly and honestly as possible in a friendly manner.

2. *Informational communication.* When people shift from social to informational communication, such as when two colleagues begin discussing work shortly after greeting each other, the content of the conversation increases in importance. Here, the primary purpose of communication is conveying information or factual knowledge. Examples would be a professor lecturing to students, a salesperson explaining a product to a customer, or a TV newscaster giving the news.

Appropriate listening at this level involves an accurate reception of the information. One begins by paying closer attention to what the speaker is saying. But it also involves processing the information for meaning and retention. If one is listening to brief bits of information, such as an appointment date or street address, mental rehearsal may be sufficient to retain the data, though a written note insures accurate retention. But when it comes to listening to more complicated information, such as a lecture or detailed production order, accurate listening requires writing down the information. Specific techniques for organizing one's material may be helpful in increasing the effectiveness of your memory (see Chapter 7). Reflective listening skills may also be useful in listening for information. Responses which paraphrase, clarify, or summarize the speaker's message serve further to check on its accuracy and meaning.

3. *Expressive communication.* In expressive communication, people use words mostly to express their emotionally colored opinions, attitudes, and feelings—for example, people sharing their grief, close friends sharing a happy experience, or customers airing their complaints. Partners attempting to resolve problem situations such as a labor dispute or marital conflict usually find it helpful to listen to a lot of expressive communication as a way of coming to understand each other's position.

Nonreflective listening may be appropriate for expressive communication as long as the speaker feels an urgent need to ventilate strong emotions. But gradually, as the intensity of feelings subsides, a speaker feels more of a need to be understood and accepted. At this point, reflective listening skills are more appropriate as a way of communicating empathetic understanding. Reflective listening is especially appropriate when someone with a problem seeks you out as a "sounding board" for understanding or a decision. Empathetic listening is indispensable when you are having a misunderstanding or conflict with someone. Instead of succumbing to the temptation to say "I understand how you feel," it is better to *demonstrate* such understanding through a specific empathetic response.

4. *Persuasive communication.* Here the speaker is attempting to persuade the listener to do something. This could come in the form of a simple request to change one's mind or attitude toward something, or it could be more of an action-oriented response, such as making a donation or serving on a committee. Some examples would be a son or daughter asking permission to go on a weekend trip, a salesperson explaining the advantages of a product or service, or a politician asking for your vote.

First of all, an appropriate response to persuasive communication means getting a clear understanding of what is being asked of you. This is where reflective listening skills play an important role. With a brief request, a simple paraphrase helps to clarify or confirm what is wanted and avoids misunderstanding. When the request is more complicated, however, additional reflective listening techniques such as clarifying, reflecting, or summarizing responses can be used. When persuasive communication is accompanied by heated emotions, as in a complaint, nonreflective listening may also be helpful, especially in the initial phases of the conversation.

Once you are clear about what is being asked of you, it is appropriate to "close the loop" of listening with some specific response. This is especially important in the area of sales, marketing, and service, where the speakers are clients or customers, often with specific expectations. When a salesperson or manager says something like "I'll get back to you on this," and nothing happens for weeks, the client wonders if that person really heard the message or simply forgot. Closing the loop of listening doesn't necessarily mean you agree with the speaker or must do what is requested. But it does mean giving a definite acknowledgment that you understood the request and are responding in some concrete way.

Since communicating takes energy and effort, people usually do it for a purpose. The better you and I can discern someone's purpose in communicating to us, the more appropriately we can listen to that person. For the most part, we do this quite well, intuitively, guided by past experience. But we also make mistakes. We have all had the experience of misunderstanding someone because we thought the words came across as social communication, when really they signified a much deeper level of feelings. As a result, we listen rather superficially when we should be listening empathetically. Or perhaps we respond to someone's persuasive message too quickly, only to discover later that we should have used active listening to find out what they really wanted.

Even though we do not consciously pay much attention to the purpose of communication, we take our cues from a number of things. A person's role and relationship to us often determines his or her purpose in communicating. In many instances, the setting or circumstances play a major role in communication. In other instances, factors such as personalities, specific occasions, or common problems are understood to govern a speaker's purpose.

But, by the same token, it is easy to overestimate these conditions. We hear what we expect to hear, from individuals and in familiar situations, so that a message that is not typical in a given context often goes unheeded or misunderstood. When we suspect that this may be the case, it is wise to ask ourselves, "Why is this person speaking to me?" "Why am I listening?" "What is the person trying to tell me?"

SOME DOS AND DON'TS OF LISTENING

Whatever the purpose of communication, good listening habits are always in order. Throughout the book we have presented many principles and techniques for improving your listening habits. Now, partly as a way of summarizing them, here are some suggestions for becoming a better listener. While many of these suggestions pertain to a specific act, such as paying attention, others involve our attitudes and motivation. All of them require repeated practice for mastery. And as you practice your new skills, it will be helpful to refer back to these suggestions.

When listening, try to *do* the following:

1. *Become aware of your own listening habits.* What are your strong points? What are your faults? Do you judge people too quickly? Do you interrupt too often? Which roadblocks to communication are you most likely to use? Which do you use most frequently? A better awareness of your listening habits is the first stage in changing them.

2. *Share responsibility for the communication.* Remember that it takes two to communicate—one to talk and one to listen—with each person alternating as listener. Whenever you are unclear about what a speaker is saying, it is your responsibility to let the speaker know this, either by asking for clarification or actively reflecting what you heard and asking to be corrected. How will someone know you do not understand unless you say so?

3. *Be physically attentive.* Face the speaker. Maintain appropriate eye contact. Make certain your posture and gestures show you are listening. Sit or stand at a distance which puts you and the speaker at ease. Remember that the one who is speaking wants an attentive, animated listener, not a stone wall.

4. *Concentrate on what the speaker is saying.* Since we have a short attention span (less than one minute) listening requires deliberate concentrations. Try to minimize situational distractions, for example, a TV or ringing telephones. Be alert for wandering thoughts. Being physically attentive and verbally responsive will probably help you concentrate on what the speaker is saying.

5. *Listen for the total meaning, including feelings as well as information.* Remember that people communicate their attitudes and feelings "coded" in socially acceptable ways. Listen for the feelings as well

as the information. For instance, the worker who says "I am all through with those letters" is sending a different message from the one who says "Thank goodness, I have finally finished those damned letters." Although the content is similar, different feelings are being expressed in the latter message. A sensitive listener who responds to the feelings as well as the content of the worker's message before making another work assignment will achieve better communication than one who simply assigns another job.

6. *Observe the speaker's nonverbal signals.* Since much communication is nonverbal, pay attention to the body language as well as the words. Watch the speaker's facial expression, and how much he or she gazes and makes eye contact with you. Listen to the speaker's tone of voice and rate of speech. Notice how close or far away the speaker sits or stands. Does the speaker's body language reinforce or contradict the spoken words?

7. *Adopt an accepting attitude toward the speaker.* An accepting attitude on the listener's part creates a favorable atmosphere for communication. The more speakers feel accepted, the more they can let down their guard and express what they really want to say. Any negative attitude on the listener's part tends to make a speaker feel defensive, insecure, and more guarded in communication.

8. *Express empathetic understanding.* Use active, reflective listening skills to discover how other people really feel, and what they are really trying to say in terms of their own frame of reference. Empathetic responses not only express our acceptance of the speaker, but give us a more accurate understanding of the intended message.

9. *Listen to yourself.* This is essential for being able to listen to others. When you are most anxious or emotionally aroused, you are least able to hear what others are saying to you. On the other hand, when you recognize the feelings stimulated in you by another's message, and can express those feelings, this clears the air and helps you to listen better.

10. *"Close the loop" of listening by taking appropriate action.* Remember that people often speak with the purpose of getting someting tangible done—to obtain information, to change our opinion, to get us to do something. The acid test of listening is how well you respond to the speaker's message with an appropriate action. In listening, as in love, actions speak louder than words.

While the emphasis should be on positive suggestions for improving our listening habits, it is helpful to keep in mind some of the pitfalls of listening.

Consequently, in listening, *don't* do the following:

1. *Don't mistake not talking for listening.* People who remain silent aren't necessarily listening. They may be preoccupied with their own thoughts. On the other hand, people can talk a lot and still process information and listen quite well. Ideally, we should be able to alternate talking and listening in an easy, natural manner.

2. *Don't fake listening.* Whenever you try to fake listening, your disinterest or boredom inevitably shows up in your facial expressions or body language. More often than not, fake listening comes across as an insult to the speaker. It is better to admit that you cannot listen at the moment, perhaps because of haste or some other pressure.

3. *Don't interrupt needlessly.* Although most of us frequently interrupt each other during social communication, those in positions of power, such as parents, teachers, managers, or executives, tend to interrupt more without realizing it. Men are more likely to interrupt than women. If you must interrupt someone in a serious conversation, try to follow with a retrieval—helping the speaker to reestablish the train of thought.

4. *Don't pass judgment too quickly.* As we have seen several times throughout this book, this seems to run against the grain. Humans have a natural tendency to judge, to evaluate, and to approve or disapprove what is said. Yet such judgmental remarks invariably put others on the defensive, serving as barriers to good communication.

5. *Don't make arguing an "ego-trip."* Even if you argue only "mentally" with what the speaker is saying, you tend to stop listening and look forward to your turn to talk. When you begin to argue verbally, you become so preoccupied with justifying your own views that you often fail to hear the other's viewpoint. How often during an argument someone will say "That is what I have been trying to tell you." When you honestly disagree, you need to listen carefully in order to understand what you are disagreeing with. Then state your point of view.

6. *Don't ask too many questions.* Occasionally, you may find it helpful to ask a question to clarify what is said. But closed questions that require a definite answer should be kept to a minimum. Even open questions that encourage a speaker to elaborate on a point should be used with caution. Too many questions have a way of shifting control of the conversation to the listener, putting the speaker on the defensive.

7. *Don't ever tell a speaker "I know exactly how you feel."* This remark serves more to justify your own efforts than to convince someone you are really listening. In the first place, it is difficult to know just how another person feels. Then too, such a generalized remark is likely to distract the speaker from further efforts at self-expression, as well as cast doubt on your own credibility as a listener. It is usually more effective to *demonstrate* you have heard with a reflective, empathetic response such as "You are feeling disappointed," "You are feeling hurt," or whatever the case may be.

8. *Don't overreact to emotional words.* When you are listening to someone who is emotionally overwrought, be careful not to let yourself get so caught up in the speaker's outburst of feelings that you miss the content of his or her message. Be alert for loaded words and expressions, but listen also for the message that comes with them. Your own feelings can block your understanding of something you may really need to hear.

9. *Don't give advice unless it is requested.* Nothing is so unappreciated as unsolicited advice. It says more about your need to help

than being helpful. Even when someone asks your advice, it is better to use reflective listening skills to determine what that person really wants to know. Otherwise, you may make the same mistake as the mother who, when asked by her small son "Where did I come from?" launched into an elaborate lecture on human reproduction, only to be told at the end, "Oh, Billy said he came from Chicago, and I just wanted to know where we came from."

10. *Don't use listening as a way of hiding yourself.* Passive, insecure people sometimes rely on "listening" as a way of avoiding communication and thus self-exposure. They are not listening as much as not talking. They are withholding their own views of feelings for fear of disapproval or criticism. In this case, people may use the appearance of listening as a way of avoiding emotional involvement and real communication. Ironically, the "listener" who uses silence as a personal retreat is inadvertently *preventing* good communication, rather than furthering it.

THE RISKS OF LISTENING

Listening, as presented up to this point, is a positive skill, which benefits everyone involved in communication. Listening has value in producing a desired action, a favorable resolution of a problem, or a new level of interpersonal relationship. Accurate listening is somtimes responsible for preventing an accident or saving a life. Listening can make or break a financial deal.

So if we say that listening is risky, you might well be surprised. Yet, listening presents risks as well as rewards. At this point we will consider some of the risks of listening, and why people avoid listening, either consciously or unconsciously.

1. *In the first place, listening makes us more vulnerable to the deeper concerns and problems of others.* Ordinarily, we filter out these things through selected apathy, as mentioned earlier. That is, we feel we have enough on our minds from our own personal lives and intimate associations without listening to others. When we really

listen to others, however, we become aware of their inner world, their needs, their aspirations, their frustrations, and their hurts. And the more we listen to people, the more emotionally involved we become with them. This also makes us more vulnerable to their feelings and problems, which, when coupled with our own, may overburden us. Then, too, since good listening requires an emotional concern without excessive emotional involvement, there is always the danger that we will exceed our tolerance for concern and compassion.

2. *Listening also increases the risk that we may see ourselves as others see us.* Each of us has built up certain pictures or images of ourselves. Some of these pictures are pretty realistic, others less so. When we listen to others, we run the risk of hearing things that conflict with those self-images. When others' views are unflattering or critical, it becomes difficult to hear, much less accept, their views of us. When we feel it is very important to hang on to a given picture of ourselves, we may become very anxious and refuse to hear what others are saying about us.

Fortunately, listening also makes us aware of the positive ways others view us. Listening helps us to broaden our picture of ourselves. We may learn that others admire us more than we thought, or feel that we are much more competent or likable than we thought. While each person's views need to be judged by the source, because of the tendency to project oneself into others, a consensus of others' opinions of us can help us to see ourselves more realistically, though it may hurt some in the process.

3. *Effective listening increases the risk of hearing criticism.* Perhaps this is why we listen so selectively in the first place. Ordinarily, we hear what we want to hear, or what we need to hear. When we have worked very hard to accomplish something, we become so emotionally identified with it that we are not prepared to hear it criticized. Criticism makes us anxious and defensive, as if we were being personally attacked.

Yet, genuinely listening increases the risk of hearing criticism. As one mother put it, if you really listen to your kids, be prepared to hear some things you do not want to hear. That is simply part of good communication. In fact, if you are in any position of authority or intimacy and are only hearing pleasant things, you should question how well you are listening. Remember, there is a natural tendency for people to pass judgment, to evaluate, to approve or disapprove.

Despite the unpleasantness, criticism may help us to correct offensive or problem behavior. It may also help us to improve our relationships with others, sometimes to the point of saving our job, our marriage, or even our life. Listening to criticism may also help to improve our performance. Many competent people regularly seek out constructive criticism as a way of improving their performance, despite the fact that criticism in itself is rarely pleasant.

4. *Then there is always the risk that we will be changed by what we hear.* When we really listen to others, we run the risk of learning new things which may change our views. Or, when we really listen, we may see others in a new light because of what we have learned about their intentions or circumstances associated with their behavior. As a result, we may change our attitudes toward other people, despite all the previous avowals to the contrary. As an old cliché goes, "to understand all is to forgive all." Perhaps that is why people in trouble tend to say things like, "Let me explain" or "If you only understood." That is, if we will hear their full story, we will change our minds. Although this may be true, it is often an exercise in self-justification. If you have made up your mind about someone, you are not likely to change it—unless, of course, you are determined to listen attentively and empathetically to that person's story. Can you risk having an attitude toward someone changed? Listen, and it may happen.

5. *Finally, there is always the risk that our listening may be unappreciated, if not exploited by others.* Ordinarily, people feel understood so seldom that they are most responsive to genuine listening. In fact, people often have to pay someone like a psychologist or psychiatrist to listen to them. Yet most people take listening for granted. This is especially likely when we are emotionally aroused, deeply hurt, or so blinded by our emotions that we may make unreasonable

demands on anyone who cares enough to listen to us. Then there are the compulsive talkers—those who express their insecurity and need for control through excessive talking—who are constantly talking, making it practically impossible to listen to them. Experience with these people soon teaches us that being a martyr does not make us a good listener. Rather, listening is hard work and must be done selectively.

THE REWARDS OF LISTENING

The risks of listening, however real, are more than offset by the rewards. Consider the following rewards of listening.

1. *Effective listening provides us with more accurate information.* In an age of spectacular electronic advances, we are constantly bombarded with information, from the television, telephone, newspapers, magazines, and conversation. Yet, because of our natural tendency toward egocentric thinking, much of this information "goes in one ear and out the other." Listening helps us to process the information we desire more effectively. When we listen with understanding, we are more likely to retain what we hear. One way to know more is to listen more effectively.

2. *Empathetic listening gives us a better understanding of other people.* Listening helps to counteract the common tendency to judge others prematurely. It may help to avoid the "we-they" orientation that corrodes human relationships. When we listen to others empathetically, we come to understand them "from the inside out." We realize that the meaning of their behavior is more complex than it often appears. We learn how people are influenced by their circumstances—their past, their relationships, their needs. We come to understand how they feel about themselves, and how they often intend to act differently than they do. In short, empathetic listening helps us to realize that others are more like than unlike ourselves, and allows us to deal with their mistakes and failures with more compassion.

3. *Listening also facilitates self-discovery.* Through listening to others we learn to listen to ourselves. We become aware of feelings, needs, and attitudes which we were only dimly aware of before. Listening may also help to broaden the picture we have of ourselves. We may discover that we are more competent, admired, or envied by others than we realized. Sometimes, of course, we will hear less flattering things, which may bring anxiety or even anger. Yet, listening to criticism may be the most helpful of all, especially when it is well intended. Even criticism given in anger may bring needed awareness of our oversights, mistakes, or faults. When taken to heart, listening is a valuable means of self-discovery and can improve our relationships with others.

4. *Listening facilitates good communication with others.* As we have said throughout this book, we must listen as well as talk if we are to move beyond the kind of "one-way" communication that invites frequent forgetting and misunderstanding. Empathetic listening creates a favorable climate for others to express themselves openly and honestly. Through reflective and empathetic listening, we learn what others are really saying, the meanings and feelings expressed in their words. We also learn how we are being heard, how others are interpreting our words. In addition, when people feel they are listened to, they not only adopt a more favorable attitude toward us, they are also more likely to listen to us in turn. Thus, listening facilitates a *mutual* exchange of information, ideas, and feelings, which is the essence of good communication.

5. *Listening also leads to better decision making and problem solving.* Decisions and solutions to problems are only as good as the information upon which they are based. Good listening helps us to process information more effectively, to take in more relevant data, and to see a problem situation from many different views before reaching a judgment. Through listening, we learn how others view the same situation, what they regard as the main problem, how they feel about it, and what they think is needed. Even though you may reach a different judgment, listening helps you to become more aware of the underlying problems as well as surface issues and to reach more satisfying solutions to problems

6. *Finally, listening may lead to better management.* Studies of workers in various types of industry have shown that supervisors and managers with good production records give a proportionately greater amount of their time to supervisory functions, including the interpersonal aspects of their jobs. One of these studies has shown that supervisors of high-production groups differed from those in low-production groups in that they:

1. were more employee-centered than production-centered.
2. encouraged employee participation in decision making.
3. spent more time in supervision and less time in straight production work.
4. had greater confidence in the supervisory role.
5. knew where they stood with the company.[2]

The truth of the matter is, the higher one goes in the chain of responsibility in business or any other field, the more one's job has to do with people and problems of human relations. Supervisors and executives alike discover that getting a job done requires respecting people as persons. People want to have a say in what they are doing, and to feel they are listened to. Those in positions of management, in addition to their special knowledge and expertise in a given line of work, must also become a special kind of people adept in dealing with others and human relations problems. "The development of oneself as a listener," says Carl Rogers, "is a first step in becoming this special person."[3]

To list all the advantages of listening would involve itemizing the functions of management itself. Listening is obviously useful for managers dealing with their bosses, for managers dealing with other managers, for managers dealing with their subordinates, and for staff people dealing with line people, and vice versa. It is also appropriate for a variety of other purposes, including the following:

[2] "Productivity, Supervision, and Employee Morale," Human Relations, Series 1, Report 1. Ann Arbor, Mich.: Survey Research Center, University of Michigan. In *Communication for Management and Business* (2nd edition). Norman B. Sigband. Glenview, Ill.: Scott, Foresman and Company, 1976.

[3] Sigband, *Communication*, p. 576.

- Interviewing: especially for hiring, firing, and making transfers.
- Motivating employees: discovering the causes of dissatisfaction, absenteeism, or turnovers.
- Order-giving: Insuring that people understand orders, as well as getting reaction to and acceptance of orders.
- Resistance to change: gaining acceptance of new techniques and procedures.
- Evaluation: discovering how employees are performing and helping them to correct their weaknesses.
- Settling disputes: Finding out the causes of disputes between employees and helping them to reach a settlement.[4]

Earlier in this book we pointed out that listening is the communication skill first learned and most often used. Yet it is the least taught and least mastered. Consequently, most of us waste a lot of energy in ineffecient listening. The results are misunderstood communication, dollars wasted through mistakes, hurt feelings, and sometimes even the loss of lives. But it doesn't have to be this way. Each of us can become a better listener. Throughout the book we have explained how to listen more effectively through gaining greater awareness of your listening habits, adopting a more accepting and empathetic attitude, and using the appropriate techniques of listening. If you *want* to become a better listener, you can do so. Apply your new understanding of listening to your everyday listening habits, and practice your listening skills until you acquire enough self-confidence to use them naturally. All of this takes time and effort. But the rewards of good listening will make all your efforts worthwhile. Good luck!

EXERCISES

LISTENING APPROPRIATELY. Below are two columns. The one on the left lists the four major types of human communication, and the one on the right lists many types of appropriate listening and responding. You are to match the two sets by writing beside each type of communication the types of listening appropriate to

[4] Leonard R. Sayles and George Strauss, *Managing Human Resources* (2nd edition). Englewood Cliffs, N.J.: Prentice-Hall, Inc. 1981.

that kind of communication. You may use some numbers more than once. When you are finished, refer to the section on Appropriate Listening on page 106 for the correct matches.

Communication	Listening and Responding
	1. summarizing
Social _____	2. active listening
	3. closing the loop
Informational _____	4. friendly
	5. avoid misunderstanding
Expressive _____	6. taking notes
	7. expressive response
Persuasive _____	8. empathizing
	9. superficial response
	10. paying close attention
	11. paraphrasing
	12. casual response
	13. passive listening
	14. memory
	15. clarifying
	16. reflecting
	17. ritual response
	18. silence

APPLYING THE TEN "DOS" TO YOUR OWN STYLE. Go back to the list of the Ten Dos of Listening on page 111. You are to select first the rule or rules that you *always* observe naturally, then those that you observe only *sometimes*, and finally those that you *never*, or almost never observe.

- Always:
- Sometimes:
- Never:

Give an example from your own experience of a rule that you observe only sometimes. Can you practice that rule until it becomes a habit?

Now give an example of a rule that you never, or almost never observe. Try it out the next time you have an opportunity, and continue to practice it until you have adopted it as part of your listening style.

ELIMINATING THE TEN "DON'TS" OF LISTENING. This is the same as exercise 2, with the terms reversed. List the "don'ts" that you *never* commit, if there are any, then those you commit *sometimes,* then those of which you are *always* (or almost always) guilty. Give examples from your experience and select one that you want to work on until you can eliminate it.

Remember that a faulty habit in listening, as in anything else, can be eliminated if you allow enough time and patience. Your work on the Dos and Don'ts of Listening can be combined. As you work to establish a new listening habit or rule you will also be eliminating a fault, that is, as you become *more* understanding you will also become *less* judgmental.

RISKS AND REWARDS. In your experience can you think of a time when you were unpleasantly shocked by something you were told? Responding to your disbelief, the person said to you, "I was trying to tell you that all along, but you wouldn't listen to me." Perhaps it was your spouse, perhaps someone at work, who was trying to persuade you to modify some behavior or expressing a complaint—as gently as possible—nevertheless, it was a warning that you did not pick up. By not listening to the unpleasant message, you merely postponed the inevitable shock. Rather than trying to forget this experience, which would be very natural, perhaps you can use it to help you discern similar warnings in the future, by closer, more attentive listening.

Now try to recall another conversation in which you *did* listen attentively and were rewarded with an enjoyable experience. Perhaps a son or daughter had been trying to talk to you about a problem at school. Instead of passing it off because you were busy, you sat down and listened empathetically for as long as was necessary. Not only did you and your child both feel better afterwards, but the way became clear for a solution to the problem, because you had listened.

Whether it is an experience at home or in some other setting that you recall, can you specify just what it was in your response that made the crucial difference? Some situations turn out well in spite of mistakes, but here you are asked to pinpoint the dominating influence on the positive side. Was it your attitude, a momentary good feeling, or did you perhaps have a twinge of conscience at the thought of not listening in that situation? For whatever reason, the success of your effort reinforced you, encouraged you to try that particular approach again when the opportunity arose.

INDEX